Practical Data Migration

The British Computer Society

The BCS is the leading professional body for the IT industry. With members in over 100 countries, the BCS is the professional and learned society in the field of computers and information systems.

The BCS is responsible for setting standards for the IT profession. It is also leading the change in public perception and appreciation of the economic and social importance of professionally managed IT projects and programmes. In this capacity, the society advises, informs and persuades industry and government on successful IT implementation.

IT is affecting every part of our lives and that is why the BCS is determined to promote IT as the profession of the 21st century.

Joining the BCS

BCS qualifications, products and services are designed with your career plans in mind. We not only provide essential recognition through professional qualifications but also offer many other useful benefits to our members at every level.

BCS membership demonstrates your commitment to professional development. It helps to set you apart from other IT practitioners and provides industry recognition of your skills and experience. Employers and customers increasingly require proof of professional qualifications and competence. Professional membership confirms your competence and integrity and sets an independent standard that people can trust.

Professional membership (MBCS) is the pathway to Chartered IT Professional (CITP) status.

www.bcs.org/membership

Further Information

Further information about the BCS can be obtained from: The British Computer Society, First Floor, Block D, North Star House, North Star Avenue, Swindon SN2 1FA, UK.

Telephone: 0845 300 4417 (UK only) or +44 1793 417 424 (overseas)
Email: customerservice@hq.bcs.org.uk
Web: www.bcs.org

Practical Data Migration

John Morris

 BCS

The British Computer Society
Publishing and Information Products
First Floor, Block D
North Star House
North Star Avenue
Swindon SN2 1FA
UK
www.bcs.org

ISBN 1-902505-71-9

British Cataloguing in Publication Data.
A CIP catalogue record for this book is available at the British Library.

All trademarks, registered names, etc. acknowledged in this publication are to be the property of their respective owners.

Disclaimer:
Although every care has been taken by the authors and BCS in the preparation of the publication, no warranty is given by the authors or BCS as Publisher as to the accuracy or completeness of the information contained within it and neither the authors nor BCS shall be responsible or liable for any loss or damage whatsoever arising by virtue of such information or any instructions or advice contained within this publication or by any of the aforementioned.
The views expressed in this book are of the author(s) and do not necessarily reflect the views of BCS except where explicitly stated as such.

Typeset by Tradespools, Chippenham, Wiltshire.
Printed at Antony Rowe Ltd., Chippenham, Wiltshire.

Contents

List of Figures and Tables

Author

John Morris has over 20 years' experience in IT working as a programmer, analyst, project manager and data architect. He has worked as an independent contractor for the last 10 years and in that time has worked for some of the biggest names in IT consultancy including CSC, Logica CMG and Price Waterhouse Coopers (PwC). He specializes in data migration and integration and for the last eight years has been involved with large-scale migrations at blue chip clients like Barclays Bank, National Grid Transco and the BBC.

Foreword

As the email asking for a foreword dropped into my email account, I was being asked my opinion on a migration strategy for moving from one HR system to another. There were several hundred thousand resource records. One major driver for this system change was that the user community did not trust the system – too many data quality issues.

As I listened, I feared that all the data problems and issues would be migrated across in all their nastiness. The result would be a continuation of poor management information and of the culture of mistrust. This was not the desired result. It was not listed in the business benefits the Board would expect after they had agreed to spend several million on this system change.

This migration strategy, like so many others, was simplistic and the path was clearly visible – littered with political bear traps, rotting corpses of ambitious consultants, and the side-lined executives who had been involved in the last big migration role waiting for someone new to join them.

However, the enthusiastic Strategy Director was convinced that this largest of telecoms companies should follow the usual system migration route of a tablespoon of well-intentioned experience and a teaspoon of some notion of best practice, mixed in with a pinch of invented migration methodology, all baked in the latest proprietary extract, transform and load software package.

I have been involved in large corporate IT for several years, seeing blue chips struggle pitifully against the vast collections of variable quality data. I have witnessed them not being able to identify any migration bridge over the information technology river.

And as a result I have seen migration strategies fail, and the resultant systems reduced to 'swearware' before the implementation team have left site.

Data migration is never an easy task. It is seen either as 'black box' activity or as a low-skilled, low-level role. But that is because the majority of consultants and technicians are scared: scared of the data, scared of the quantity of data, scared of the quality of data, and scared of the amount of work it takes to get it right.

So my admiration is extended to John for writing this text. He has taken the best of all of his experiences as a Migration Consultant to define a technologically independent and unique methodology for managing a successful data migration based around his four Golden Rules. And he has taken the worst of his experiences to list the pitfalls to warn his fellow migration journeymen.

I for one will be recommending this book to clients, large and small, who face a data migration, to both prove that they can do it successfully and gain real business benefit from their activities.

Chris Harrold
Director, iergo
www.iergo.net

Glossary

audit trail	An audit trail is a record of the actions carried out on the data as it progresses through extract, transformation and loading.
Check Points	Check Points (also sometimes known as 'go/no go points') are the decision points where it is agreed that the new system is stable enough to go forward with or from which Fallback occurs.
churn	Churn is the relative frequency with which records of different types are added, amended or deleted from a data store.
Conceptual Entity Model	A Conceptual Entity Model is a form of data model where atomic entities are grouped together to form higher-level entities that are meaningful to the enterprise.
Control Total	A Control Total is either the sum of some meaningful value within the data being transferred or a count of the number of records being transferred.
Data Architect	Terms like 'Data Architect' are bandied about a lot in IT and can mean subtly different things in different departments, from an extremely technical role related to the nuts and bolts of databases and servers to a more widely encompassing one. A good working definition is 'The Data Architect is responsible for the design of how the data required for an organization, possibly held over multiple applications, is held' (from BCS' Careers Leaflet CWG13). Corporate Data Architects will have an overview of how the data is structured and where it is mastered in those common cases where the same data item is used in more than one place. They will also be responsible for producing, and often enforcing, institution wide definitions of key enterprise entities.
Data Freeze	The prevention of updates to records after they have been extracted for data migration and before they are loaded into the new system.

Data Mapping	A Data Mapping is the rule by which one or more data items in a Legacy Data Store will have their values moved to one or more items in the new system database.
Data Quality Rules	Data Quality Rules are a statement of the metrics that will be used to measure the quality of the data for each of the data sets under consideration, either at Legacy Data Store or Key Business Data Area level, and the set of steps that will bring current data to the level where these metrics are met.
data size	Data size is the amount of data to be loaded.
Data Stakeholder	A Data Stakeholder is any person within or outside the organization who has a legitimate interest in the data migration outcomes.
Data Transitional Rules	Data Transitional Rules are the temporary business operating procedures put in place to cope with the disturbance caused by data migration itself.
Fallback	Fallback is the group of steps that will be taken to get the enterprise back into the position it was in prior to the data migration.
Fallback window	The length of time between starting up the new system and taking the final Check Point that allows for the full decommissioning of Legacy Data Stores according to the System Retirement Policies.
homonym	Two words that are spelt or pronounced the same way but have a different meaning. In a business context the word 'account' will mean something different to a salesman and an accountant.
Key Business Data Areas	A Key Business Data Area is made up of those Legacy Data Stores and enterprise functions that physically hold the data for a significant entity on the enterprise's post-implementation conceptual entity model.
Legacy Data Stores	A Legacy Data Store is a data repository of any type that holds data of interest to the new system.
'One Way Street' Problem	The 'One Way Street' Problem arises as a result of any algorithm that transforms data in such a way that the original values cannot be retrieved.
run time	Run time is the length of time to execute a data migration extract, transform and load program.
sequencing	Sequencing is the ordering of update processes into a tenable progression.

synonym	Two words that are spelt differently but have the same meaning. In our example the terms 'equipment' and 'machine' can mean the same thing.
System Retirement Policies	A System Retirement Policy is the specification and plan for how a Legacy Data Store will be decommissioned.
transaction	A transaction in IT is the full set of database updates, applied in the correct sequence, that are needed to accomplish a business task.
Transient Data Store	Transient Data Stores are temporary databases that are created during the process of data migration. They are needed for a variety of reasons, but should not be allowed to persist beyond the lifetime of the data migration project. They can be as sophisticated as a fully normalized enterprise-strength database or as simple as a spreadsheet.

Preface

This book has been a long time in the writing. It has been over eight years since I first got directly involved with large-scale data migration. Although I suppose with a data architect background it was bound to happen sooner or later, I was still amazed, when I came to it for the first time, how easy it was to go wrong.

Struggling, I sought in vain for an instruction manual. It was not to be found.

We have Unified Modelling Language to help us model our new systems, we have Prince to manage our projects and we have, well who knows how many methodologies to choose from, to identify and manage our requirements analysis. But getting the right quality of data out of existing repositories and into our shiny new systems? We are left high and dry.

It is remains a fact, however, that every system needs new raw data to start it off. That data has to come from somewhere. And if we want to realise the value of our investment then we want the right data, of the right quality, delivered at the right time. And isn't maximising the return on our investments what we are all about?

Eight years ago, when I first wrestled with the problem of extracting and merging data on a corporate scale, I realised that there was this gap in the methodologies. I could not find help in written form anywhere. Eight years on the situation is the same, until now. I swore then that I would write this book to fill that gap.

Well, as I say it took a while before I put finger to keyboard. There was always that next project to work on. And there have been plenty of those, as word spread that here was someone game enough to tackle the unpopular and messy business of locating, preparing and loading data – and someone who knew how to get it right. Each project taught me something new, but the underlying tenets of this approach have been proved right time and time again.

There have been a number of influences in the writing of this book and in the development of the method. But I will single out Nina Turner from the others because it was down to her persistence and refusal to accept second best that I was forced to realize that we needed to invent a new approach if we were not to sell our business colleagues short. It was with her that I soldiered through that first data migration to a successful conclusion.

I would also like to thank my wife, Josephine, for her help and patience as I have completed this manuscript and to my brother Christopher for his kind assistance in reading early drafts and making valuable styling and practical suggestions.

I would like to thank Philip Kogan for his initial encouragement with this book and to the publishing team of Matthew Flynn, Suzanna Marsh and Florence Leroy for making this process so painless for a novice author.

Of course, though, the ideas represented in this book are those of the author and the author alone.

I am always interested in receiving comments from other practitioners in this field and if you want to contact me drop me an e-mail to: john.morris@informationergonomics.org.

John Morris
14 December 2005

Introduction

What is the purpose of this book?

This book is aimed at practitioners, project managers and purchasers of consultant resources who have a data migration project to deal with. It is designed as a teach yourself guide to data migration. It is written by a consultant with many years' experience in data migration to give you a series of steps developed in real life situations that will get you from an empty new system to one that is populated, working and backed by the user population.

What type of data migration is covered?

Data migration projects take on many forms. The classic is where a new system is to be implemented and needs to be primed with data from the legacy systems. There are also system consolidation programmes, either spawned by businesses merging or by a drive for standardization. There are system upgrades and these also require data migration. However, whatever the spur for data migration, the same problems will have to be faced, and this book will guide you past the pitfalls.

For the sake of simplicity and consistency, unless there is a specific reason to indicate differing approaches for different types of data migration, I am going to refer to the old/existing data as the 'legacy system' and the destination as the 'new system'.

What is not covered in this book?

This book is system-neutral. It is aimed at large scale data migration projects visible to the end user population. It does not cover the detail of migrating from one version of Oracle or SAP to another. It does not cover changes to operating systems or hardware. For every change like that there are courses available and, if there is a sufficiently large market, books will emerge. This book is aimed at the gap in the methodologies that will allow you to develop the perfect system then say nothing about how you get the best legacy data out of the flaky old systems you are trying to leave behind.

This book also does not cover the regular movement of data that supports business information type applications, be they data warehouses, data marts or Management Information Systems (MIS). This book is aimed at a project environment where there is a clear need to move data as a 'one-off' to populate a new data base.

> **Hint**
>
> A project is a one-off enterprise event with a beginning, a middle and an end. A business process is cyclical, individual items will move through from the start event to the final transformation but the process itself never stops. Know the difference. Projects require different management skills from processes, have different deliverables and different timelines, but it is surprising how easy it is get the two confused. Superficial similarities hide the essential differences.

Having said that, there are techniques in this book that can be used to perform data analysis and data cleansing and that can be used to bring the enterprise into the project, so it may still be useful reading for anyone interested in cyclic data cleansing or data quality issues.

Who is this book aimed at?

There are two types of reader who will find this book essential reading – the executive and the practitioner.

The first will be the person with management responsibility for seeing the project to a successful conclusion. You may be a practising or a lapsed technologist, but you want to know how to control a data migration project.

The second is the technologist with the prospect of a data migration project looming in front of them and sensibly reaching for assistance.

The executive

You may be surprised to learn that there are no non-proprietary (ie not tied to one particular technology or consultancy supplier) methodologies for data migration. In other words no one has created a widely accepted series of steps that will guarantee to get your dirty old data out of your old systems and transform it into clean new data to be placed into the new system in which you have invested so much of the company's money.

Well there is now.

This book will demystify the plethora of terms with which we technologists love to surround our activities. It will illustrate the sort of controls you should expect to see from a well-managed data migration project. It will illustrate the steps you should expect an experienced data migration consultant to execute. So if you are responsible for hiring consultancy resources or are overseeing an in-house project, this short book will arm you with the ammunition you will need to stay on top of the project.

I have also put in a series of alerts when the book, necessarily, enters technical areas that, perhaps, a controlling executive need not know about. Look out for the health warnings!

The practitioner

If you are a practitioner about to embark on a data migration project for the first time (or even second or third time) you are right to feel daunted by the scale of the task. Bad start-up data is the curse of many a good project. It is not a subject that is well covered in most computing courses. It might not even seem that glamorous. Well, do not worry; follow the methods and principles in this book and you will be guided to success. You will even make lasting allies out there in the real world of your enterprise.

Because this book is also intended for the executive you may, occasionally, find yourself being told things that are the common currency of your daily working life. I will attempt to warn you but I would advise you to stick with it. Data migration uses many commonplace concepts in subtly different ways.

Worked example

Throughout the book I will be referring to a worked example. Now although this is based on a real migration carried out under real pressures of time, cost, access to the right people etc, I have had to reduce the complexity radically or I would have been at serious risk of losing my audience. The real project had scores of Legacy Data Stores and the new system had hundreds of tables. I have had to retain sufficient complexity to allow the examples to work, but if you can see the right answer sometimes without going through all the steps, well you'll have to trust me that in the real world it just is not that simple! I am also aware that in simplifying the model some of the relationships seem pretty banal and a moment's thought will allow even the slowest amongst us to realize that a system built like this would probably not satisfy anyone.

In essence the migration problem could be expressed as:

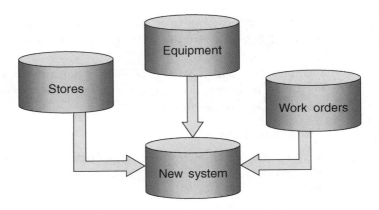

FIGURE 0.1 *Worked example of the basic problem*

An enterprise decided that in place of the separate legacy applications they had holding their items of equipment (held in the fixed asset register), a system (or more properly dozens of systems) raising work orders and a stores application holding work equipment, they would invest in a single application. One of the drivers for this decision was the acknowledged problem that the asset register was not being maintained properly because there was no enterprise driver for the people in closest contact with that information – the army of engineers and fitters – to update what was seen as an accounting overhead. On the other hand the lack of uniformity meant that in different parts of the enterprise wholly different maintenance practices were in place. This had led to wholly different costs.

I am using it as an example for a number of reasons.

First, and most significantly, I think most of us, whatever our backgrounds, can understand a work ticket and an equipment item. We've all had a car or washing machine repaired. A more esoteric example drawn from the arcane world of banking or finance might not be so intuitively obvious.

Second, those of us who have been through any kind of data analysis course will be familiar with the 'parts explosion' – where one piece of equipment is made up of many other pieces of equipment. It's an interesting example to play with when we get to the decision-making aspect of just where to draw data items from and how to map one item to many others.

And third, and perhaps selfishly – it means I get to use some of my most pithy anecdotes to enliven and illuminate the text. It was doing just such migrations that I served my apprenticeship. Even if since then I have broadened my scope, it was in the first couple of outings that I made most of the mistakes that you will avoid if you follow my advice.

Paragraph styles

To make the text easier to follow I have adopted a number of style devices. I have split the book into instructional text – this will appear in paragraphs like this one.

There are also:

Anecdotes

These record real life experiences and, hopefully, illustrate the point I am making in the main body of the text.

Hints

These are tricks and tips that I have found to work. These should, of course, be applied with circumspection based on your knowledge of the culture and structure of the environment in which you are working.

There will also be:

Golden Rules

You will be introduced to four Golden Rules that underlie and govern this approach. They are the most significant things to take away from this book. Learn them by heart and, whatever else you find expedient to change, stick with them and you will have increased your chances of success many times over.

And there are:

Definitions

As well as the Golden Rules there are also other key ideas, unique to this approach, that need to be carefully defined. So that you can find them again easily later, they are in boxes like this.

Additionally each chapter will start with a quick overview of what is inside and conclude with a résumé of what you should take away with you from that chapter. The overview will look like this:

In this introduction you will be told the scope and purpose of this book and its intended readership. You will be given an indication as to why following this approach will increase your chances of success.

And the chapter review will be like this:

Chapter review

This chapter explained:
- *what types of data migration are intended to be covered by this book;*
- *who the intended readership is;*
- *what the worked example looks like;*
- *what paragraph styles will be used to guide you through the book.*

Part One
Reasons and Methods

1 Reasons

In this chapter you will be given the reasons why data migration matters:
- *the positive benefits of a well-run data migration exercise;*
- *a cautionary tale of what a data migration project going wrong looks like.*

WHY QUALITY DATA MIGRATION MATTERS

Traditionally the Cinderella of information technology (IT), tagged on at the end of the project plan, data migration can be the difference between benefits realization and lost opportunities. Data migration is not just about moving data from one place to another; it should be focussed on:

- realizing all the benefits promised by the new system when you entertained the concept of new software in the first place;
- creating the improved enterprise performance that was the driver for the project;
- importing the best, the most appropriate and the cleanest data you can so that you enhance business intelligence;
- maintaining all your regulatory, legal and governance compliance criteria;
- staying securely in control of the project.

But first a cautionary tale of how things can go the other way. This is told from a practitioner's perspective but can be read just as easily from an executive's point of view. It is just that the executive is likely to know that things are going wrong only towards the very end of the story, when it is clear, to even the most optimistic, that a good result is just not going to happen. Anyone who has been involved in this area of work will recognize many of these symptoms. Use this book wisely and they need not happen to you.

A PRACTITIONER'S PERSPECTIVE

OK, so you've drawn the short straw. You've been given responsibility for migrating data into the exciting new system your colleagues are busy delivering. Whilst they are having all the fun you will be chasing after them getting data ready to populate their new system. This part of the programme has started late. You do not have access to any of the new tools that your colleagues do. There appears to be nothing in any methodology that will help.

It may be that you have never done anything like this before. Or worse, you still wake up in the middle of the night sweating about the last time. You know: that time when the data was not clean and some of it was missing. What was there was inadequate and after months of effort the users still criticized you for re-creating errors that had previously been removed from the legacy system. But then you never had the time or the resources to do what you needed. It just seemed like one long hopeless panic. Not surprisingly, the system go live was delayed. Masses of data items were rejected then cleaned, then re-entered, only to be rejected again. The users expressed their unhappiness through senior management and it all cascaded down onto you.

In the end something went live but the first few months were a fraught period of firefighting data errors that constantly compromised the system.

Well stop worrying. Follow the steps in this book and the users will love you, the programme manager will buy you lunch and you'll be an all-round hero.

I may be exaggerating a little. Chances are that if you do a perfect job no one will notice. Get it wrong and then you become the centre of attention. I mean loading data is easy right?

Wrong. There are lots of ways of getting it wrong. There are many traps out there waiting to be fallen into. I know, I've fallen into most of them. What follows is the distillation of 20 years' hard won experience.

Critically I will show you how to retain enterprise ownership of the data migration process. All too often the data migration process begins with the technology and ends in disaster. Follow the steps outlined in this book and you will tie the enterprise into the success of the migration project from start to finish.

I will guide you through a series of steps that will guarantee that the data loaded meets the enterprise's requirements to the enterprise's complete satisfaction. You will be on time and to budget having built sustainable bridges with the enterprise community.

But first a short tale of how, typically, it can all go wrong...

A new system has been defined, modules are being delivered and the launch date is approaching. The programme manager sees from her plan that it's time to build the data migration scripts. Given the other issues she sees this as easy. It's only a matter of a business analyst and a couple of coders. Go out, speak to the users, analyse the existing data, define the shape of the new data, maybe draw up a few data models to help, then onto the data mapping spreadsheets. When those are completed and signed off by the users, you will get the coders to write the migration scripts, then it's testing, loading and away you go.

Better still, perhaps you have been provided with a new migration tool.

This allows you to capture data structures and transformation rules and produces the code for you.

And of course the new system has a data import facility. You're not quite sure how it works but the salesmen seemed confident that it has all been done before somewhere else.

Of course there is that slight worry about the previous legacy migration whose data never really fitted into the current systems. And one of the users did mention a spreadsheet that was used for some reporting. You told your line manager but he pointed you to the signed-off specification that tells you, explicitly, where the data is going to come from. If there is a secondary use of system data in a spreadsheet then that is an issue for the reporting team.

You also recall one of the users, in passing, mentioning the special use of one of the date fields but you recorded the fact and are confident that you can sort it out in coding.

Time is now running short and things are going to be a bit tight. The original systems analysis overran and the development team is having problems with some of the interfaces, so your coding resource will be two weeks late. But you re-plan and, given the signed-off data mappings, you feel that you should make it. You warn the programme manager at this stage that the delay in resources is a risk but she has more urgent budget problems to deal with so you wait.

Eventually your programmers arrive and coding starts. The load scripts all work well with the test data generated within the team, just the usual collection of bugs to weed out. You breathe a sigh of relief and go about the task of securing a cut of real data from the legacy system.

Then the first hint of the disaster that is about to overwhelm you, and the project, appears. A perplexed programmer arrives at your desk to tell you that 10,000 of the target records failed to load out of a population of 20,000. Scaled up, that would mean half a million records being dumped out at system load time. The programmer can't understand it. The code worked with her test data. It must be a data problem. You will have to go back to the users.

As you are digesting this piece of information a second thunderbolt strikes. Your other programmer appears at your desk. He has uncovered a data gap. A vital link needed by the new system does not appear in the old. But how could this happen? For the enterprise to operate this link had to be made and look, there is the linking table. So how can the linking table be empty, or worse still, only part-populated?

This is the point, when you look back at the end of the project, that you can see that your projected end date was doomed. For now, though, you still feel that given good will and hard work and maybe longer hours you can recover the situation. You raise a couple of issues on the programme issue register and go back to the users for assistance.

You find them strangely unco-operative. Sorry they have no resources to spare, they tell you. Everyone is committed either to the day job (and don't forget, it's the day job that pays your wages) or to training for the new system or to user acceptance testing. They certainly do not have, at this short notice, the staff to hand-load half a million records, and as for referential integrity – that is clearly a technical issue. You took on the problem of data loading and it is up to you to sort it out. And as you are here, was user acceptance testing not expected to have been started by now?

You return to the programming team to be told that the situation is worse than they expected. Whilst they have been waiting for a response from you, they have been delving into the live system. There are at least another five serious data errors in the legacy systems that make it impossible to locate the correct record types. The projected number of rejected records is now approaching a million and rising. Also, mysteriously, some of the required data seems to not be present in the legacy system. Do you have any ideas where it might be?

The programmers sit across the desk from you, arms folded. They are technicians, they explain. They do not know the meaning of the data items, only the rules by which they should be linked. It is an end user data problem, they declare.

Then the phone rings and it's a worried programme manager. She has just been called into the office of the Chief Finance Officer. What's this about the regulatory reporting system and why is it not being migrated? Could you look into it please? You have a vague recollection of those spreadsheets. Didn't they become part of the reporting team's responsibility? Oh no they didn't, you are told. They hold crucial information that was re-entered back into the legacy system via an Open DataBase Connectivity (ODBC) link and have to be replicated in the new system. The company's statutory financial reporting depends on them.

The final straw occurs when the small amount of user acceptance testing that you have managed to do, just to keep the user population happy as you try to fix the data issues, reports back. An old bug, fixed four years ago, has reappeared. The tester is apologetic but he knows that his boss will never sign off a system that takes the enterprise backwards. She wasn't even all that keen on having a new system anyway.

Need I go on? I could add a dozen additional scenarios of how the technology-led approach can, and in all but the most simple of cases will, fail. Of course, most projects struggle on to some form of conclusion. Usually in the form of a 'live' system that limps through its first dozen or so weeks, more often down than up as 'data glitches' mysteriously crash the otherwise perfect functionality.

The users blame the project for the additional, unplanned work loaded on them and for the poor quality data in the system they get in return for all the promises. The project blames the users or more specifically the users' data, for the delays in the project end date. This is reflected in their reports to the project steering committee. This of course further alienates the user population. Time scales are extended. Functionality is postponed. Additional project phases are added and the original business case is compromised. The end of the project descends into a spiral of mutual recriminations, disappointment and damaged careers.

Does any of this sound familiar?

Perhaps you are engaged in just such a heroic struggle right now and are reaching for help. Well if so, even if it may be better to never get into that situation in the first place, this book will hold pointers as to how to get the project back on track – but, man, is that hard work. Skim through the book first to get to grips with the terminology and techniques then go to Part Three, Rescuing Data Migration Projects. And good luck to you, I know what you are up against. I've been there myself!

If you have witnessed just such a project disaster and are now dreading a reoccurrence, then take heart. Let this book be your guide and you will sail through the project to the rapturous applause of you peers and the undying affection of the user population.

But why do these problems typically appear? A clear specification was produced. The users signed it off. How could these data issues appear at the last moment? How could the enterprise have operated previously with such poor quality systems? Why did no one tell you about the other enterprise-critical systems out there that needed attention? They weren't in the original specification were they?

The truth is that in today's complex, client server environment, with constantly shifting enterprise structures and personnel, there will be no one person that does know how the enterprise operates. The programme's original business analysis will have uncovered some variation in working practices but this information is not, typically, passed on to the data migration team.

Local initiatives will also frustrate the data migrator. In today's client server desktop environment, with departmental computing budgets and a fair degree of native computer skills spread unevenly across the enterprise, local solutions will be found to business problems. These will typically not be documented and are almost certainly unknown to the centralized IT functions. We have to remember that on a big legacy system there have been thousands of man years of labour invested by the user population in attempting to make their enterprise function work smoothly.

Frequently, fields that are used for one purpose in one part of the company, at one point in time, may have a completely different meaning elsewhere or at different times.

The degree of skill and intelligence that has been applied to the company's business will also vary from business centre to business centre and from time period to time period. All this will be reflected in the data as we find it at migration time.

There will also be damage caused by long forgotten bugs, and their fixes, compromising data quality.

So as you sift through a company's legacy data remember that you are looking, not at a static collection of fields, but at the representation of that thousand man-years of effort (and not all of it well directed).

This book will show you how, by applying tried and tested techniques, to get all this hidden knowledge out of the enterprise and into the project and, as importantly, how to get and retain enterprise sponsorship and support through a difficult and stressful period for both sides.

The key to a successful migration is to remember that data migration is a business not a technical problem and data quality is a business not a technical issue. It is for the enterprise to dictate how and where data comes from and goes and what constitutes sufficient data quality. It is our jobs, as handmaidens of progress, to assist with the technical issues of moving data from one place to another, identifying referential integrity and other technical issues, and facilitating the process. But we are the servants not the masters.

Another way to look at it is that too often we start from the wrong question. We ask 'How are we to migrate this data?' instead of asking 'What data should we be migrating?' The first is a technically focussed question, the second an enterprise-focussed question. By confusing the two we, on the technical side, take responsibility for the choice of data items and this is a responsibility we do not have the knowledge to carry.

Chapter review

In this chapter you have been told that:
- *data migration projects are inherently difficult;*
- *data migration projects should be enterprise- not technology-led;*
- *there is a series of steps you can take to minimize the difficulties;*
- *those steps are contained in this book.*

2 The Golden Rules

In this chapter you will be introduced to the four Golden Rules of data migration. These underlie all the other activities in this book and are the single most important set of concepts in the book. Study them, learn them and live your data migration project by them.

THE MOST IMPORTANT LESSONS

If you take nothing else from this book, take these rules to heart and use them to inform your migration activities. If you follow all the steps laid out below, to the letter, then I guarantee that you will deliver quality data to your users' total satisfaction. But I am also aware that in the real world, in which we IT professionals live and work, there are always local cultural, commercial and practical realities that constrain our freedom to act as we would like. Almost any of the forms and steps below can be replaced by something more suited to the environment you find yourself in (I'm not saying that a substitute will work as well as the tried and tested advice I'm offering, but I acknowledge it may be expedient). However, whatever formats you operate in, abandon these Golden Rules at your peril. Each one is essential and collectively they form the underlying philosophy of this approach. Abandon these rules and you are on your own!

These four basic principles will make the difference between a successful migration, with which the enterprise will be happy, and a tortured chain of actions that lead to recriminations, customer dissatisfaction and even failed projects.

They are not always easy to communicate, however. Some are challenging. Stick with them as you proceed through the rest of the book and they will make sense in the end.

Golden Rule 1

Data migration is a business not a technical issue.

This is the first and most significant rule. This may be counter-intuitive to both the technologists on one side and the enterprise on the other. Data migration normally occurs as a result of an IT project and because we in IT are attracted to technology, we tend to look for technical solutions. That is why there are data cleansing and loading tools in the market place. However, this is putting the cart before the horse. IT projects are there to answer an enterprise need. The enterprise understands the meaning and relative value of its data. It is this value that must be preserved and enhanced in the transformation activity that is data migration. It is from this knowledge that data cleansing, data preparation and extract, transform and load definitions can be derived. We, the technologists, can see the bits and bytes, but we are dangerously arrogant if we think we can see the enterprise meaning of those bits and bytes better than the owners, creators and users of them.

Anecdote

I first got involved with data migration because a project I was working on had a big data take on requirement. Fully half the migration budget had been expended building a migration environment. The users rejected this as unusable because, in their eyes, it was not targeted at the main data problems. So after going through the thick end of £250,000 we were running late with no data and no idea where we were going to get the data from.

The technologists were backing away from the problem. After all they had built a perfectly good tool hadn't they? The design document was all signed off wasn't it? The users were losing patience with the technologists. Why weren't they being listened to?

I was intrigued. We had clearly gone about this the wrong way, providing a solution before we had understood the problem.

We migrated successfully in the end but the migration tool was never used. It was the start of the process that led, after much trial and error, to the set of procedures I'm sharing with you now.

This is not to say that there is no technical element, but let us look at a typical migration strategy

You are called into the boss's office and told that the new system will be ready in a matter of weeks and could you get the data loaded? Often technical resources are made available to you. But where is the data and how well does the old fit the new? Again this always seems obvious. It is in the legacy system. So we go ahead and specify load programs, write them and test them in the clean environment of the development office. Then we come to the first test load, and it all goes wrong. Half the data is missing, defects known to the enterprise but not formally acknowledged come to light, and suddenly a plethora of new data sources are revealed. We are now running late and the recriminations start.

One of the reasons for this problem is that back in the good old days of mainframes, no one could do any data processing outside of the control of the IT department. But oh, how times have changed. In the anarchy of the client server world, each IT-literate individual in each department will have their own set of spreadsheets and mini-databases. Some, totally unacknowledged, will be crucial to your enterprise's processes, often filling in for the inadequacies of current systems (and if they are not inadequate, why are they being replaced?). Each will be different in format and quality and there may be no matching keys. Of course, no one will have told you about this. Often senior management will be unaware of, or uncomfortable to share, this fact. And, given the silo nature of enterprise structures, the view of the user data the project has will be that of the senior managers.

a

Anecdote

The largest number of individual data sources I have encountered on any one site runs into the low hundreds. We narrowed it down to 74 from which we wanted to gather data. And, yes, we had been told in advance that all the information we needed was in three corporate systems.

And look at it from a user perspective. You have arrived with all your technical arrogance and assumed responsibility for loading their data. They do not hear anything for a while then suddenly a flood of data that will not load is cascaded back at them. They flounder in the deluge without tools, mechanisms or resources to cope.

At this point something significantly bad will have happened to the IT–enterprise relationship. The enterprise had accepted the passive role offered it. The IT department had suggested that it had the technology and the tools to migrate the data from A to B. The IT department were confident that their technology could cope. Suddenly the dastardly enterprise is providing data in entirely the wrong format. The elegantly written and executed software will of course throw out the errors. The implicit contract between enterprise and IT has gone wrong. You have misled one another. The enterprise was expecting to be getting on with the day job whilst the technologists got on with the data. Now a lot of extra work is coming their way. This wasn't what was promised! Expectations are undermined and relationships descend into a spiral of mutual recriminations.

But why? The reason is, of course, that there has been a subtle (often, in politically charged environments a not-so-subtle) shift of responsibility. The data loaders have, in the eyes of the enterprise, taken on the responsibility for getting existing data into the new system. And that includes cleansing and preparing the data. The data loaders, however, know that they do not have the knowledge, and often do not have the access permissions, to correct errors and inconsistencies in enterprise data. The contract between the two parties is floored by being founded on a basic misunderstanding.

It might seem easy to correct this but in my experience, with modern, lean, efficient companies and departments whose key personnel may have been pulled around considerably in the development process, it can be extremely hard for a compromise to be reached. Bad feeling persists which ruins any co-operation that may have existed and will make it doubly difficult in the future.

The answer is to stick closely to Rule 1. From start to finish the enterprise must own the quality of the data and the success of the migration outcome. After the final programme day, when we all pack up and head off onto our new projects, it is the enterprise that must live with the results.

This does not mean that there is no room for technical competence. We must still specify, write and test our programs carefully. We still have a role to play in guaranteeing the technical appropriateness of the new data. But long after we have all moved on to our new projects the enterprise will be stuck with what we have given them. Follow the steps outlined below and the enterprise will be enthusiastically tied into the successful outcome of the project.

Hint

To help overcome any resistance to retaining ownership of the data migration process in the enterprise, stress the spin-off value of learning how to initiate data quality improvements. These same techniques can be used after implementation to continually enhance enterprise data quality. It's an early and easy win.

Golden Rule 2

The business knows best.

This follows on from Golden Rule 1. The enterprise is the expert in what the enterprise does. The enterprise has been running the legacy systems, and the legacy systems have been running the enterprise. Within the enterprise there is the knowledge of where all the data sources that secretly run the enterprise are located. The enterprise has within it all the experience and expertise to make valid judgements as to quality and appropriateness of data items.

Anecdote

I was consulting to a company in a heavily regulated industry on changes needed to satisfy the regulator. At a presentation to senior management, I was asked what the consequences would be if I failed to successfully migrate some of the data because of user resistance. I replied, in line with

Golden Rule 2, that if the enterprise ultimately judged that they could forgo the data quality the regulator demanded for sound enterprise reasons and were prepared to stand up to the regulator, then I was not in a position to disagree. It was not my data. I owned neither the process nor the result. It was a hard point to make but after that there were no more challenges on the issue of ownership.

It would seem obvious, probably the least challenged of the Golden Rules. But it is vital, as you will see, to the rest of the method that we never stray from this obvious truth. It is all too easy, in the hurly-burly and time pressures of a typical data migration exercise, for sight of this to be lost. Even with the best will in the world, lots of consultation and plenty of well-written documents signed off, there is still a risk that the technicians will start to take responsibility for decisions. It may seem expedient, it may seem low risk, but it never helps in the long run. This is not an issue about the quality of the decision. The technical decision may be correct. This is about ownership.

However we, as technicians, do have value to add to the process. We know about the technical difficulties involved with matching different data formats. We know about normalization, common points of reference and identity. We know how to transform data and how to create Transitional Data Stores for data cleansing. We know how to extract, reformat and import data. We can perform gap analysis and we can facilitate the process.

And facilitating the process is important. Although the enterprise knows best, this knowledge is usually scattered throughout the enterprise. One of our main contributions must be to bring out of the enterprise that knowledge and allow them to do the very best job that time and money will allow with what they have. The approach in this book has a number of techniques designed to do precisely this.

There are different types of knowledge that we have to unearth. Using the concept of Data Stakeholders introduced in Chapter 3, we will learn how to identify those different types of knowledge and how to satisfy them. We will learn how to harness the various layers of ownership to our mutual advantage.

But always, always, in everything we do, we must acknowledge that we on the project cannot know more about the enterprise rules than the enterprise does itself.

Golden Rule 3

No organization needs, wants or will pay for perfect quality data.

This is the most challenging assertion in the book, but one of the most important. So many data migration projects are unsatisfactory because there was an unspoken driver at the outset to enhance the data quality of the legacy system to a level approaching perfection. So what is wrong with this as an aspiration?

Well our personal experience tells us this will not happen. The typical project profile is one of high expectations at the outset, followed by a series of compromises en route. Budgets and schedules start to slip and then there is a mad dash for the finish. Data migration, often being at the end of the time line, is the phase of the project that suffers most by this time and cash squeeze. It is the quality of the data that becomes compromised, as time gets short. It becomes a case of getting what you can instead of what you would like.

Compound this with the change in ownership that breaking Golden Rule 1 brings. Focus on the wrong data sources by breaking Golden Rule 2 and, on go live, the enterprise user is faced with a system with all the inherent problems of the legacy they thought they were getting rid of, plus a few more.

Worse still, both sides – the technical and the enterprise – feel betrayed. From an enterprise perspective the technical will have failed to deliver on the implicit promise to produce perfect quality data and will then be perceived as arrogant and out of touch with the needs of the 'real' enterprise when the compromise data is placed before the user population. From a technical perspective the enterprise will have failed to tell the technical side all the details of their legacy systems and will be throwing up a series of late challenges to the go live date.

What normally happens then is that the project descends into mutual recriminations, and responsibility for securing data of even sufficient quality to run the new system from day one is pushed back and forth across the divide between the two sides of the enterprise. The next project down the pike will find itself mired in the backwash of this history of problems.

Because data quality compromise is our experience as the norm, let us plan to accept it from the outset.

The starting point is to be honest up front. Get the message across about Golden Rules 1, 2 and 3 from the beginning of the project. Again, there are practical steps outlined below that will tie in the enterprise and get the right compromise decisions made in good time by the right interested parties.

You will always find that in the modern slimmed-down enterprise, the enterprise has interests other than the project the reader of this book is working on.

- Executives have many calls on their time.

- Middle managers are squeezed by the cascades of initiatives tumbling down from above and the demands of their staff bubbling up from below.

- Frontline staff are too busy with the day job to provide extensive support for non-operational work.

These are the inevitable facts of enterprise life. Add to them that the project will have a life of its own, with a fixed end date, and it is easier to persuade that compromises need to be made once the issues are fully understood. Accepting this in advance means that sensible, considered priorities can be drawn up. Leaving it until budget and time are running out leads to rushed, ill-considered decisions based on expediency not utility.

Be honest from the start. Lay out the issues. Accept up front that there will be compromises. Structure the relationship so that the enterprise decides what to prioritize and what to drop. Just as importantly, the enterprise should be able to put a brake on any developments that limit its legitimate operation.

This book will show you how to structure a data migration project so that these issues are confronted early and dealt with smoothly. A series of project deliverables will be produced that will ease the technical–enterprise relationship from one of confrontation over an implicit contract to the co-operative partnership that will better deliver what the company wants and needs.

a

Anecdote

I was working on a management information system some years ago for an emergency services organization. I had thought, in the circumstances of a large incident, with loss of life and property and the consequent legal issues that might arise, that nothing could be lost. I was wrong. There were many details that were captured on some system or another that were not of any interest. For instance the mobile cafeteria system recorded when particular types of rolls were sold on its point of sale systems. It is getting the information that matters to the enterprise out of the mass of data that is important. And who knows what constitutes meaningful information? That's right, Golden Rule 2 – the business knows best.

This point was best made for me when I was working as a consultant at a large, national organization, and an engineer who had been working on a data migration sub-project presented me with a diagram (see Figure 2.1). It neatly encapsulates the degrees of information that are available in most organizations and the choices that have of necessity to be made.

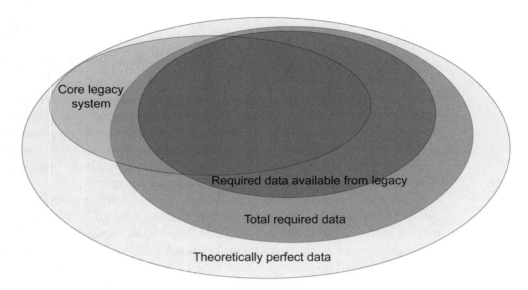

FIGURE 2.1 *Sufficient for purpose data*

Golden Rule 4
If you can't count it, it doesn't count.

Almost without fail, when I join a project and ask about the data quality I will be told 'It's quite good in system x' or that a particular database is 'poor quality'.

Similarly, when I ask what data quality threshold is required in the new system I will be told that the enterprise expects 'excellent' or 'very good' or even 'perfect'.

But when I ask how are we going to know if we have achieved these targets I am met, often, with a blank stare. Well-managed projects have measurable deliverables and a data migration project is no exception. We need to be able to report on percentages complete. We need to be able to compare disparate potential data sources. We need to be able to perform gap analysis. To do that with accuracy we need to be able to measure our achievements and the size of gap between where we are and where we need to be. We need hard facts about our data that we can measure. Anything else is aspirational waffle.

This method will show you how to drive out these measures and how to record them. By basing their creation on Golden Rules 1 and 2 they will be the measures that make most sense to the enterprise.

Chapter review

In this chapter you have been introduced to the four Golden Rules of data migration:

1 Data migration is a business not a technical issue.

2 The business knows best.

3 No organization needs, wants or will pay for perfect quality data.

4 If you can't count it, it doesn't count.

Learn them. Write them out and stick them on the wall above your desk. And whatever else in this method you choose to compromise, depart from them at your peril.

3 Data Stakeholders

In this chapter you will be introduced to:
- *the concept of Data Stakeholders;*
- *how to identify Data Stakeholders;*
- *generic types of stakeholder;*
- *how to get them to commit to their role.*

INTRODUCTION

We have seen from Golden Rule 1 that a data migration exercise, to be successful, must be enterprise-led, which is an easy thing to say, but is often difficult to put into practice. We technologists would much prefer to keep our heads down and get on with the closely defined task of moving bits and bytes around rather than the messy and possibly confrontational business of gaining ownership. But you have to tackle this task early in your project, when motivation and enthusiasm are high, or risk trying to find ownership later when major issues need to be resolved.

Identifying Data Stakeholders is not just about building alliances before things get tricky later on in the project, however. It is central to an enterprise-led approach to data migration. If saying that data migration is a business not a technical issue is to have any meaning then we must find those people in the enterprise who will provide direction to our project. As you will see below, this is not about something as vague as some data champions, these are well-defined structurally significant roles.

It is also important to have allies in the enterprise that will get the tough decisions made and help you through crises when you need them. If you wait until the crisis breaks before looking for help, finding those allies will be a whole lot harder. People naturally tend to run for cover when disaster looms. What you are building here is a virtual team. You need enthusiasts and experts at many levels. And these experts are generally to be found out there in the real, everyday world of the enterprise.

There is also the question of ownership. As soon as you create your first mapping table you will have taken ownership of the data migration project. Once you gain ownership it is difficult to move it back to the enterprise. This is especially true if you wait for issues to emerge. Remember, you must avoid the implicit promise that the enterprise is going to have a passive role in this project. The enterprise must own the ultimate delivery and the solutions to problems you will encounter along the way.

THE COMMUTER AND THE KNIGHT ERRANT

There are two models that I use to illustrate this point – the quest and the train journey.

On the latter you sit passively in your seat and watch as the world slips by your window. The journey is in the hands of the train driver and he, in turn, is depending on an unseen army of track engineers, signalmen, overhead linesmen and rail engine mechanics to get you smoothly to you destination. If you have any contribution to the success of the journey it is limited to purchasing a valid ticket and turning up on time. When things go wrong you vent your spleen on the driver and the incompetence of the rail company. And quite rightly so. You were not involved with the process of getting from start to end, only with the choice of destination itself.

Now imagine a quest. It is more exciting but fraught with the possibility of failure. There may be a leader but each participant is expected to contribute, to a greater or lesser extent, to the success of the venture. On the classic quests of literature, each person brings a different set of skills to the task. The hero-leader may not even have direct command of his companions. He or she may have had to negotiate for their services and has to work hard to maintain their loyalty.

Now which of these models is more appropriate to the process of a data migration exercise? We normally imagine the train journey metaphor is the best way of managing our users. We promise to provide a deluxe service, carrying our passengers to their destination with little effort on their part. Keeping them quiet and out of our way allows us to get on with the technical aspects of the task unhindered (and gets us out of the potentially embarrassing problem of having to deal with all those messy political issues). Having to explain our esoteric decisions to the uninitiated can be awkward.

But is the train trip an honest metaphor? We know from experience that there will be problems along the way. These problems will only be resolved with the assistance and experience of those people most immediately involved with the legacy systems. Even if everything goes smoothly we know that at the end of the process we will be asking them to sign off that their existing systems can be decommissioned and that their new system is fit for purpose. The train journey metaphor breaks down before we reach the destination. We do not buy a ticket then expect to have to sign off that the railway is fit for purpose before we are allowed to reach our destination.

On the other hand the quest metaphor is quite apt. There will be trials and tribulations along the way. The ultimate sanctioner of the success of our epic will not be the hero-leader of the quest, but either one or a collection of local panjandrums. Unexpected problems and challenges will beset us, and compromises will be needed as well as possibly heroic efforts. Dragons will need to be slain and beautiful princesses will need to be rescued...

OK, so maybe I am exaggerating a little, but I still contend that the model of the passive train journey is floored from the outset. We are misleading our users and ourselves if we suggest that they can have such a non-active role in the project. We know it will not be that way, we know that at some point we will have to come clean. If we think about it for a minute, we also know that having come clean, our users will feel misled.

They will feel misled because they have been misled. We have not been honest with them. We gave them to understand they were going to have an easy ride and now we are asking them for a much more significant contribution. When the train inexplicably stops, or when delays occur, as passengers we sit and curse the 'others' who we hold to blame. We may not know who they are, but we know for sure that it is not our responsibility. We do not expect to have to do anything to fix the situation. Fixing is someone else's problem. This, though, is how we treat our key enterprise contacts in a typical data migration exercise. We tacitly imply that their role will be limited then spring a huge surprise on them mid-way through.

On the quest, however, although we may know that any one problem may be someone else's fault, we are still all bound into the overall success of the adventure. We see ourselves as part of the solution not as passive observers of the problem. And if we have the skills, or even if we do not, we will try to make a contribution to the success of the project.

The key difference is that in the one model we are only bound into the success of the journey's end. In the other model we are joint owners of the process by which the journey reaches its end, as well as owning the success of the journey's end.

ⓐ

Anecdote

Allowing the enterprise to become too dependent on the technical side in a migration exercise can have bizarre results. I worked on one migration where, in a population of 12,000 records, seven records needed special processing. Instead of going ahead with the migration and picking up the seven records later for manual action, the enterprise side looked to the technicians to write special code to deal with them. Emails flew around, deadlines were missed, meetings were held and load windows compromised. Had the enterprise properly owned the migration a more commonsense approach would have prevailed (as indeed it did in the end, but not without an unnecessary amount of pain). As it was, the dependency culture meant that the issue was seen as a technical problem not a business problem. As an enterprise problem both the technical and manual solutions would have been considered and the more appropriate action taken earlier and more cheaply.

OWNERSHIP

Finally there is the question of ownership. We on the project should not own the sign-off of the project. The enterprise should, and almost always will, have the ultimate go/no go sign-off responsibility. They have the power to qualify your efforts as a success or a failure. They should therefore own the problem of data migration as well as its results.

An industry standard approach is for the technical side to propose a solution. This is formally documented and the document is signed off. We then use the document as evidence in any disputes. As I showed in the introduction, disputes are almost certain to arise so this document becomes key.

Such an adversarial approach is inimical to progress. Multiple meetings will be arranged and issues will be escalated to the highest authorities in the enterprise, all of which wastes time and money. Costly change control procedures will be invoked. Documents will be rewritten and reissued. Plenty of projects founder on just these cycles of rejection and re-work.

It is also ultimately self-defeating because the power, in most companies, does not lie with the IT department. If what we prepare is not fit for purpose, producing documentation that shows we built to specification only serves to antagonise and alienate our colleagues. It will not make the solution any more acceptable. We will end up re-working it or both sides will have to settle for a messy compromise that satisfies neither. In my experience, if it comes down to an argument, especially in a data migration exercise, the signed-off specification will be of little use. Your work will be rejected and will have to be re-worked. Only now you will have a less co-operative and more antagonistic set of users to deal with.

I am not suggesting that we do away with formal documentation. As you will see, everything you do will be formally sanctioned by the enterprise, but the documentation we produce is more flexible and does not attempt to prescribe in advance what may not be discovered until later in the time line. Because, however, the enterprise is intimately involved with the decision-making at each step of the way, the cost, time and design implications of each decision will belong to the enterprise.

Hint

I always make it a mantra on a project that power should not be divorced from responsibility. Because the enterprise has the power to accept or reject the solution, the enterprise must take responsibility for that solution.

FINDING THE RIGHT FELLOW TRAVELLERS

OK, so we have agreed that the quest metaphor is more apt. We need to create alliances with the enterprise communities where the knowledge lies and with those who will ultimately sign off our activities. To do this we need to identify our Data Stakeholders.

> ### Data Stakeholder
>
> **A Data Stakeholder is any person within or outside the organization who has a legitimate interest in the data migration outcomes.**

This definition is important. Taking the definition in reverse:

- Projects are about outcomes (or 'deliverables') more than processes. The physical coding process may belong to the techies but if, for example, an audit trail (see page 51) must be shown to satisfy a regulator then this must become one of the outputs and must be reflected in the project processes.

- A legitimate interest is harder to define and will vary from project to project. There are some mandatory Data Stakeholders that must be identified for each data source, but otherwise it is usually better to be inclusive rather than exclusive.

> ### Hint
>
> **We have all worked on projects where some well-thought-of employee takes an informal interest in all projects, dipping in and out almost at whim. These people can be quite disruptive. Get them to define their legitimate interest – possibly an architectural one. Usually it is better to have them inside rather than outside, but if you want to be rid of them, remember Golden Rule 1. Once you have got buy-in from your key Data Stakeholders, get the other stakeholders to assign them a role or reject them.**

- Data Stakeholders, as we will see from some of the examples below, can be drawn from outside of the organization – external auditors are an obvious example.

- A Data Stakeholder, for our purposes, is a person not a group. They may represent a larger group but we need individuals we can contact, with phone numbers and email addresses, empowered to make judgements and decisions.

We will be expecting a lot from our trusted band of Data Stakeholders and we must bind them early into the success of the project. They must know their role and accept the responsibilities that come with it. Finding all your Data Stakeholders and getting buy-in is one of your first and most difficult tasks. Below are some of the common Data Stakeholders, starting with the two that are mandatory for every data source you find.

Data Store Owner

A Data Store Owner is the individual within the enterprise that has formal responsibility for the quality of the data in a system and for its use.

> **Hint**
>
> An easy way of identifying a Data Store Owner is that they are the employees who have the power to sign off your decommissioning statement – they can sanction switching a system off.

However, finding Data Store Owners can be difficult. It may seem simple but in modern enterprises with their constantly changing structures and their wall-to-wall ERP systems, finding owners can be hard. Some systems seem to be used by everyone and owned by no one.

> **Anecdote**
>
> I was working on a project in a heavily regulated national company and the project required that I make changes to one of their key infrastructural systems. Although each module could be identified with an enterprise function, and therefore ultimately with a director, the system as a whole seemed to be owned by no one. In the end I settled for the senior business manager of the function in which I was working as my Data Store Owner. One can persist up the chain of command until you reach the CEO but you may have to settle for a committee of senior managers. Remember the key question is: 'Who can authorize that this system be switched off?'

A Data Store Owner will also be needed for the new system once it is commissioned. Often it is one of the Data Store Owners from the more significant of the Legacy Data Stores (see page 46), but sometimes the new system implementation will be going hand in hand with enterprise structural change. Find the Data Store Owner and get them signed up to their role. They will need to be party to the Data Transitional Rules and possibly to the System Retirement Policies outlined in Chapter 4.

Business Domain Expert

Frequently the Data Store Owner is not the person in day-to-day contact with the data source. The Data Store Owner may be a senior manager who has moved into their position from elsewhere and never had hands-on contact with the system.

You may find, however, that the Data Store Owner, some time and a couple of promotions ago, worked with the Legacy Data Store. This can be more difficult. They may believe that they know what is going on but beware. System use evolves with time and with personnel. You need to know how the data source is used right now, what its idiosyncrasies are and what work-arounds are in place today, not how it used to work in the past.

Hint

Just as they can be a challenge, Data Store Owners with a long association with the data source can also be an asset. They will have knowledge of the history of faults, fixes and enhancements that so often compromise data migration.

Having a long association with the data source also, normally, leads to a natural commitment to its data quality. Tell these people about Golden Rules 1 and 2, with due humility, and you will be pushing at an open door. Treat them with insensitivity and you will alienate them all too easily.

You need a Business Domain Expert that is up to speed with the way the data source is used now. This does not mean that the Business Domain Expert and the Data Store Owner cannot be the same person – they often are on small local data sources – just be aware of the degree of up-to-date knowledge you are expecting of your expert.

Also be aware of the degree of commitment you are expecting of your Business Domain Expert. This is supposed to be a co-worker on the virtual team you are building. They must be available at the end of a phone for a quick call. They must be free to attend workshops at reasonable notice. A senior enterprise manager whose diary is booked for months in advance and who has a PA to answer email is unlikely to suit.

Anecdote

Finding the stakeholders is not always simple. I was called in to consult on the struggling data migration aspects of an outsourcing programme for a large multinational financial institution. Unfortunately the project was running very late by the time I arrived on site and most of the Business Domain Experts had already been outsourced. Without them we had no way of judging if the proposed solution was fit for purpose. It took

> considerable effort to track down suitable Business Domain Experts. This is an illustration of the problems caused by failing to explicitly link the requirements of the data migration project with the wider programme.

Your Business Domain Expert may also not work directly for the Data Store Owner. You need the best person for the job that the enterprise can spare. This is another reason for taking a top-down approach. Get Data Store Owner buy-in at the outset and resourcing issues become that bit easier to resolve.

Finally, the Business Domain Expert should be just that – an expert. Do not be fobbed off with some junior that is the easiest person to spare. The Business Domain Expert will be your champion in their enterprise area. Their peers should respect them and accept that they can adequately represent the business domain's interests.

Hint

So I've just set you an impossible task – find perfect Business Domain Experts. In my experience these people are usually well known in their environment but are also often over tasked, dealing with every new initiative that comes their way. It is up to your negotiating skills and powers of persuasion to get the best you can. This is one of the reasons I recommend a top-down, enterprise-owned approach. Identify the Data Store Owner, make the situation real to them and then get them to select a Business Domain Expert after explaining the role. Never forget Golden Rule 1! If they do not prioritize your project over the others making a call on their staff then, after due warning, accept their view and get them to sign it off.

In large, complex, systems you will need more than one Business Domain Expert, each familiar with their own aspect of the data source and its use. One representative that everyone can trust, who has the internal network of contacts to get answers to questions and can select the correct invitees to meetings is better than a plethora of experts, but you may have to make a compromise between an army of experts and a lack of knowledge. Whoever is chosen, they need to be credible to the enterprise with recent, real, hands on, business domain experience.

Technical Data Experts

In anything other than a simple data source there are often aspects of the system that only the technically expert can know about. These may relate to file formats, access permissions, interfaces etc. It is usually easy to identify the Technical Data Experts. They may work for the IT department just like you do. They are often the system experts you are first pointed to when you get your initial job brief. These people are important, but not as important as the Business Domain Experts are and definitely not as important as the Data Store Owner. Do not allow yourself to be misled into thinking that the systems administrator is the same as a well-informed user of the system. They are not, but many a data migration founders on the confusion of the two roles. You will not need me to tell you that someone as closely associated with a data source and its uses as a systems administrator is a valuable source of information on who are the best candidates for Business Domain Expert. They will also be well informed on issues of data quality.

Finally, as I keep banging on, it is imperative that no matter how well informed the technical side is of the enterprise issues, a data migration project must be led by, and be seen to be led by, the enterprise. If the technical side take the lead then they will own any and all problems they find. Again, no matter how expedient it might seem to you (and to your programme manager) to use the skills of some business analyst who is the acknowledged expert in this business domain, hold out for a local Business Domain Expert.

Programme Experts

It is obvious that the programme, of which this data migration project is a part, has a legitimate interest in the data sources. It may be that you, the reader, are the Programme Expert as far as data migration is concerned. But just as the Business Domain Expert and the Business Data Store Owner are distinct roles that can be embodied by the same person, so the Programme Expert and the Data Migration Analyst are distinct roles. Do not confuse them. In any case, on a large data migration it is unlikely that one person will be an expert across the whole of the target system.

Second, confusing the legitimate interest of the programme with the interest of the enterprise causes more problems than any other single thing. As a data migration expert you are the mediator between what the programme needs and what the enterprise and other Data Stakeholders need. You must satisfy all your Data Stakeholders, not just the programme.

I cannot tell you how many data migration exercises I have been involved with that have started from the premise of programme not enterprise need – probably just about all of them! From the outset the focus is on staffing the project with people who know the target and not the data sources. We concentrate on getting the data that the target system needs over the data that the enterprise needs. Remember, data migration has (at least) two ends – a new system for sure but also a Legacy Data Store end as well.

I am not recommending here that you re-work the analysis that has gone into the target system. That has to be a given to the data migration project.

It is the choice of source, of quality and of audit trails that is the decision area of the data migration project. This is a shared responsibility with the other Data Stakeholders (along with Data Transitional Rules, retirement policies and a heap of other things that we will cover later in the book).

Corporate Data Architect

Those organizations with a sophisticated approach to data management and administration will often have an information management function where corporate data models and data architectural models will be maintained.

> ### Data Architect
>
> Terms like 'Data Architect' are bandied about a lot in IT and can mean subtly different things in different departments, from an extremely technical role related to the nuts and bolts of databases and servers to a more widely encompassing one. A good working definition is 'The Data Architect is responsible for the design of how the data required for an organization, possibly held over multiple applications, is held' (from British Computer Society Careers Leaflet CWG13).
>
> Corporate Data Architects will have an overview of how the data is structured and where it is mastered in those common cases where the same data item is used in more than one place. They will also be responsible for producing, and often enforcing, institution wide definitions of key enterprise entities.

If the organization in which you are delivering a data migration project has such a function it is extremely unlikely that you will not be made aware of it at the inception of the project. Given that these people's day job is reviewing data standards and maintaining data models, they make an extremely useful first port of call when you get onto the process of defining the Key Business Data Areas (see Chapter 4) and producing the legacy data models. They will be well informed of the data quality issues in existing legacy data, so make a good starting point for your first-cut Data Quality Rules straw men (see Chapter 5). They are the official corporate lead in best practice data design methods, so it makes sense to use their modelling standards, tools and methods. As you will see when we look at the example specimen project later (see Chapter 9) there is a section where choices of deliverables can be made. Use the advice of the local experts to choose the tools that are mandated or just work best in the environment in which you find yourself.

On a personal level, Data Architects are usually well informed as to who the best candidates for Business Domain Expert and the other key Data Stakeholders are.

However, once again there is a health warning. Corporate Data Architects do not have day-to-day, hands-on, use of their systems. They are not a substitute for Business Domain Experts. They are usually organizationally and culturally part of the IT function within the organization. And remember Golden Rule 1!

Sometimes, but rarely, they have Data Store Owner responsibilities, but again the key question of who has the final say in decommissioning a Legacy Data Store will normally resolve this issue.

The main area where there is a potential for conflict between the data migration project and the data architecture team lies in the contradiction between enforcing corporate policy with regard to private data stores and getting the best data available for the new system. Here we need to be clear about our role as data migration expert facilitators of change, not owners of the solution. I personally always push for a full amnesty over legacy data stores where these run counter to corporate policy, for the initial period of the migration exercise. However, it is often the legitimate role of the Corporate Data Architecture team to resist this. Once again it comes down to the wider business assessing the arguments in favour of the fullest possible set of data stores against the impact on corporate discipline. The worst case is to duck the issue. It has to be faced, a decision made that all parties can agree to (and possibly an entry made in the risk register).

Anecdote

Each enterprise differs in the degree of latitude it allows its staff for local initiatives. Sometimes even within the same organization there are differences. When I was working for an emergency services organization the discipline against private data stores was absolute amongst the uniformed section. Amongst the civilian workers, however, there was a greater degree of flexibility.

Once again, though, we must stick to the rules. If there is to be a Corporate Data Architecture stakeholder, they must be named, with roles, responsibilities, email addresses and telephone numbers. It may be that the way the information resource function is organized there will be separate people responsible for data modelling and physical data storage design etc. I prefer a single contact with overarching responsibility to my project, even if they pass the work around within their own department, but however it is accomplished you should have an agreed series of deliverables and methods of communicating.

Audit and Regulatory Experts

Most organizations these days are subject to external auditory and regulatory requirements. The process of data migration, both in the process itself (or more appropriately the audit trail evidence left after the process has finished) and in its delivered data, may be subject to legitimate audit and regulatory inspection. If this is so in your case then you will need a contact for each of these requirements. These contacts can be external to the company for whom you are working, but are more likely to be fellow employees who have the contact responsibility on behalf of the company. Either way, identify them if needed.

Once again it may be that the same person is your Business Domain Expert and your >Audit and Regulatory Expert. This is not a problem. As long as you can sort out when they are speaking on behalf of the user community and when they are speaking on behalf of the regulator. This is important; regulatory requirements usually take precedence over user ergonomics but it is not unknown for the two to be conveniently confused for the benefit of the user population!

Data Customers

Alongside the regulatory and audit there are often internal recipients of data – quite often information is gathered that is needed elsewhere, outside the business domain of origin. It is sometimes necessary for these Data Stakeholders to be identified. Be careful how wide you cast your net, however. Analysis of data in Legacy Data Stores can often identify additional data items that need to be passed on. The choice of appropriate Technical Data Experts should inform the project of those interfaces to secondary systems invisible to the Data Store Owner or Business Domain Expert. Bringing too many parties into the project risks making your work unwieldy, bringing too few risks oversights. I'm afraid it is a matter of judgement and experience, but, hey, that's what you are being paid big bucks for, right? Only invite those who clearly have something to add.

Other stakeholders

It is not unusual that in the environment in which you find yourself you may need additional Data Stakeholders. This is fine provided you can define their role and agree it with the other stakeholders. Beware of having too many people involved, and closely define all stakeholder roles so that their influence is not allowed to extend beyond their proper competence.

Chapter review

This chapter explained why we should approach our data migration activities as a quest for the best data that time and effort will allow. To do that we need to establish our virtual team of Data Stakeholders. Each one has a clearly defined role, from Data Store Owner to Business Domain Expert to Data Migration Analyst.

4 Four Key Concepts

In this chapter you will be introduced to the concepts of:
- *Key Business Data Areas;*
- *Legacy Data Stores;*
- *System Retirement Policies;*
- *Data Transitional Rules.*

These are unique to this approach to data migration and will be constantly referred to elsewhere. They combine to form a powerful group of tools that, if used within the spirit of the Golden Rules and in conjunction with other tools and techniques outlined in this book, can help to build a migration strategy suitable for any enterprise facing a data migration project.

FIRST: A HEALTH WARNING

This chapter uses formal data modelling and data analysis concepts that are key to understanding the data requirements of an enterprise. I apologize for getting technical, but we really cannot get any further without resorting to the use of some industry standard modelling conventions.

If you are reading this book as a programme or business manager looking to gain an overview of what a data migration project should look like then I'll allow you to glaze over as we discuss Conceptual Entity Models.

> **Hint**
>
> Along with data models you will often hear the term 'metadata' bandied about amongst the technologists. Metadata is defined as data about data. In other words, it is the data the technologists hold about the data in the business. As a technologist I use the word freely when talking to my peers. I avoid it like the plague in front of my enterprise colleagues and you will not find another mention of it in this book. There are possibly less accurate but more accessible substitutes like 'data description'.

However, it is essential that the four key concepts within this section be grasped at least in outline. If you diligently read this chapter, and the rest of the book, then all will become clear in the use of this approach.

If you are charged with the task of getting the data in, then perhaps you might be advised to go back to those dusty college books of yours and remind yourself of these concepts if you are a bit unclear about them.

Hint

Use the simplest modelling technique you can to communicate with the enterprise. This is why I recommend data modelling over the more sophisticated and possibly precise object modelling. My data models consist of a box for an entity and a crow's foot for a relationship. I also use the 'nested box' convention to represent super-entities where I want to limit the complexity of a diagram to a view that only has the entities I am interested in (see Chapter 6 for examples). This I can teach to a group of Data Stakeholders, in a meeting, in a couple of minutes and then we can have a meaningful discussion. However, I have no strong preference for any particular technique. If it helps mutual understanding, use it, whether it is object models, rich text or entity relationship diagrams; just try to avoid any technique that really requires a couple of weeks of off-site training.

Now on with the definitions!

Key Business Data Areas

A Key Business Data Area is made up of those Legacy Data Stores and enterprise functions that physically hold the data for a significant entity on the enterprise's post-implementation conceptual entity model.

On a large data migration project the data requirements of the new system will be complex. The way to tackle a complex problem is to split it down into a set of simpler problems. Data migration is no exception. I recommend that you split a large data migration project down into several Key Business Data Areas. Obviously, on less complex migrations this may not be necessary.

Key Business Data Areas are used both in the initial analysis of the Legacy Data Stores and in the subsequent fit of legacy data with new system requirements that results in the extract, transform and load definitions.

There are a number of approaches to this decomposition. I prefer to use logical entity modelling techniques (as outlined below). This is probably because my background is in data analysis, database design and data architecture design. If you feel less comfortable with this then project decomposition based on business function may work just as well. Or again, sometimes, where the new target system is modularized, it makes sense to follow the target systems modules. That way, for each Key Business Data Area the data migration project will be dealing with a single Programme Expert stakeholder.

Another consideration when creating your Key Business Data Areas is the migration forms – Big Bang Implementation, Parallel Running Implementation or Phased Delivery (see the Data Migration Implementation Forms section in Chapter 7). It could be that if you are adopting a Phased Delivery because of the geographic diversity of your enterprise, your division of activity should be along the same geographical lines. However, in these circumstances I still usually find that subdivision around conceptual entities is also still advisable at least for planning purposes even if personnel are assigned by region.

Whichever way you do it (or if you choose not to subdivide the task at all), this is a first order task. You have not looked in detail at the Legacy Data Stores as yet, so any breakdown has to be provisional. The flip side of this, of course, is that you have to be prepared to acknowledge later on that your initial decomposition was inaccurate and be prepared to change it. And late changes cost more. What you need is a usable set of work packages to plan and work within that make sense to the activities described later in this book, to the enterprise and to the wider programme. Best judgement is required I'm afraid.

USING CONCEPTUAL ENTITY MODELS TO DEFINE THE KEY BUSINESS DATA AREAS

On a data migration exercise I start from the premise that someone else has performed the data analysis and process analysis that informs the new target system. This can be taken as read. We are not interested in business process analysis because this is a data migration exercise. (This is not strictly true, as we shall see when we come to Data Transitional Rules later.) We are interested in data and comparing source and destination data structures; therefore, industry standard data modelling techniques are probably the best way forward.

I also anticipate that there will be data held in legacy sources within different business functions with different Data Store Owners that relate to the same logical entities. These will have to be brought together at load time. It is easier to control this if our project decomposition is datacentric. That way bringing together data from different sources will be controlled under the same work package flow. The alternative, of decomposing by existing enterprise functional areas, risks confusing historical, enterprise functional categories (that are usually based on business process not data structure) with data structural categories.

Of course the corollary of this is that we may find that our data-biased division is so at odds with the enterprise decomposition that we risk having all our Data Migration Analysts trying to arrange meetings individually with all of our key Data Stakeholders. We may have to temper our academic enthusiasm with a degree of pragmatism.

Finally, if you draw up an accurate Conceptual Entity Model you will expose the relationships between the Key Business Data Areas, albeit at a high level. Often the enterprise managed, by re-keying or some other manual task, to make these links work in the past. Therefore the links may not be there to be found in the data structures of the Legacy Data Stores. Your Conceptual Entity Model will help to point to the existence of these missing links.

Conceptual Entity Model-based Key Business Data Area decomposition is only a predisposition on my part. By all means make a pragmatic judgement in the light of the situation you find yourself in. I have successfully used the modules within target systems as my basis for Key Business Data Areas where that seemed more appropriate.

Anecdote

I have worked on enterprise merger activities where the key Data Stakeholders were separated both geographically and by company. There it made sense to treat each source company as a separate Key Business Data Area.

Even if you do not choose to partition your project by Key Business Data Area, I still recommend you create a Conceptual Entity Model or its equivalent. It makes the cataloguing of Legacy Data Stores much easier.

So what, in this context, is a Conceptual Entity Model?

Conceptual Entity Model

A Conceptual Entity Model is a form of data model where atomic entities are grouped together to form higher-level entities that are meaningful to the enterprise.

This definition, although correct from an academic viewpoint, is a little misleading. It suggests that we need to have a full entity model of the problem domain before we can create our Conceptual Entity Model. In fact, unless we have the benefit of a Corporate Data Architect Data

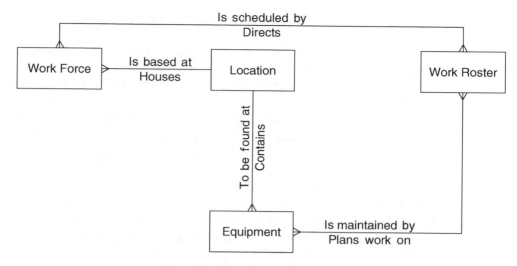

FIGURE 4.1 *Conceptual Entity Model*

Stakeholder we may have to make do with a working hypothesis. I repeat this has its risks, but we are only trying to decompose our activity into meaningful pieces.

Let us look at our worked example. Based on a quick look at the project brief it might appear that a meaningful Conceptual Entity Model might look as shown in Figure 4.1.

In my preferred way of working each conceptual entity will become a Key Business Data Area. Because conceptual entities are those that correspond to a meaningful thing in the enterprise, all the clever associative entities needed to resolve many-to-many relationships, and involuted data relationships can either be discarded or added to one of the Key Business Data Area definitions. Any overly simple conceptual entities should also be combined into one of the Key Business Data Areas. What you should have at the end of this process is a set of groups of things that make sense to the enterprise but that completely cover, and can be traced back to, the data requirements of the new system. So for our worked example we will have the Key Business Data Areas of:

- Equipment;
- Workforce;
- Work Roster;
- Location.

Already we have split one big problem into four more manageable and much smaller ones.

As we encounter the Legacy Data Stores (see page 46 for formal definition) we will cross-refer them to the conceptual entities to which they relate.

DOCUMENTING KEY BUSINESS DATA AREA RELATIONS

Create an overall model of all the Key Business Data Areas and how they relate.

If you started with my preference for a simple but formal Conceptual Entity Model then the entity model becomes your Key Business Data Area model. If you have done your job properly, even for the largest and most complex of programmes, there will be less than a dozen entities on your model and therefore less than a dozen Key Business Data Areas.

However, if you prefer, or sometimes if you inherit, a rich text diagram that the enterprise understands and you have chosen to decompose the project on the same lines, then use that. But whatever you choose, it should be printed out A0 size and stuck on the data migration project's office wall. It should appear in presentations and in documents. Your project planning will be based on it. Do not keep it secret. Publicize it, make it part of the language of the programme.

DOCUMENTING INDIVIDUAL KEY BUSINESS DATA AREAS

Ideally you will have inherited from the programme a full legacy data or object model replete with a full definition of attributes etc. If you are really fortunate you will have a Corporate Data Architect stakeholder who will provide you with both conceptual and lower level models meticulously maintained. However, I am aware that many companies' implementation methods do not require them to produce this as a deliverable. Often you will be working off a database schema and a set of mappings of processes onto system modules. Sometimes, especially where the driver for the project is business consolidation or business demerger, you may not even have an up-to-date schema. You are then confronted with a dilemma. You need the physical and the logical view of the Key Business Data Area, but do you have the skills or the time to fully develop it?

I would suggest that you need a logical data model developed at least to the extent of entities and relationships, with the common points of reference documented even if time does not allow for a full attribute level data model for each Key Business Data Area. And remember you will need one for both the legacy and the new system environment, so allow for the time (and skilled resource) in your planning and budgeting.

Anecdote

I have been a big fan of formal data modelling techniques for over two decades. Given the choice I will always go for a formal model of each Key Business Data Area and each significant data set within the Key Business Data Area (always bearing in mind Golden Rule 3). However, I was working at one very large engineering and food processing company and one of the most important Data Stakeholders just could not work with data models. I do not know why, he was brilliant in other ways, but he just couldn't 'get it'. For his Key Business Data Area I abandoned formal models and used pictures, spreadsheets and long textual descriptions to define the Key Business Data Area and create Data Quality Rules. It was harder work, it was probably less rigorous, but it got us where we needed to go. By all means try to steer the process, but remember Golden Rule 1 and where fundamental resistance is met with, go with the key Data Stakeholders' preferences and find some other route.

So document each Key Business Data Area in whatever format works best for your environment. As the project progresses, this model will be developed and used to analyse the fit of each Legacy Data Store, first with the legacy Key Business Data Area models and then with the new system Key Business Data Area models. Ultimately you will also of course need a complete physical definition of how each Key Business Data Area is to be replicated in the new system but you may not need that level of detail in the legacy Key Business Data Area models.

Hint

Although it is true that attributes define entities and for addicts of formal normalization techniques starting with the entities and working down to the attributes is anathema, this data migration method is based on getting something good enough to move forward with. We are not striving for perfection in our intermediary products. The iterative nature of our approach will catch any shortfalls. Initially we need a view of the existing and future Key Business Data Areas at an entity relationship level, so that we can uncover data gaps. It is for this reason that I tend to use top-down entity relationship analysis over bottom-up normalization.

CONFUSING DATA STRUCTURES AND BUSINESS FUNCTIONS

It is imperative that we do not confuse Key Business Data Areas with the business functions that use them. This is because there is often an overlap of business functional boundaries that use the same Key Business Data Areas for different functional reasons. Just because most organizations are functionally divided – Accounts, Sales, Production etc – does not mean that they are divided according to our data model. Our interest relates to data not to function or organizational boundary.

This confusion of functional structure with data structure causes a lot of problems. For instance the values in the Accounts are generated by, and used by, systems that are not owned by the Accounts team. At data migration time, values from these other systems may be needed to complete the migration. To do this (and identify data gaps) we need a standard of compliance of these Legacy Data Stores with the Key Business Data Areas. I recommend we do this by matching their data models.

A worked example of this process follows in Chapter 6. But first let us look at what is meant by Legacy Data Stores.

LEGACY DATA STORES

Legacy Data Stores

A Legacy Data Store is a data repository of any type that holds data of interest to the new system.

Once the Key Business Data Areas have been identified, Legacy Data Stores can be linked to one or more Key Business Data Areas. This gives us a way of organizing a plethora of candidate sources into sets that can be planned for and dealt with systematically.

Anecdote

I use the word 'store' as opposed to 'system' advisedly. It is normal to get essential fragments of data from spreadsheets, card indexes and other paper files. I have even transcribed data from hand-drawn plans dating from before the First World War. Although in an academic sense these can all be characterized as 'systems', the word 'stores' conveys a more accurate description in everyday language.

Identifying Legacy Data Stores is both hard and easy. You will almost certainly in the project brief be given a list of probable Legacy Data Stores. Use this as your starting point but expect there to be other Legacy Data Stores out there that are possibly known only to a few.

Hint

I start migration projects with a well-publicized amnesty on the revelation of private data stores, whatever the corporate policy on private data stores may be. I also put a strict deadline on the amnesty after which change control is rigorously enforced.

Be as inclusive as possible. It may only take a few minutes to dismiss a data store as being entirely derivative and not important but it can cost you the price of the whole programme if a key data store is overlooked.

It is also discourteous to dismiss a data store out of hand. It would be arrogant to assume that we know better than an employee how the company is run. Welcoming, not dismissing, the input of local knowledge is another way of building that wider virtual team that will deliver the project.

Hint

If it happens that you do reject a data store that you subsequently find is needed, be honest and open about your mistake. There is nothing that will build teams better than being prepared to accept an 'I told you so' lecture because your response should then be: 'Yeah, you were right, now what are *we* going to do about it?'

Expect additional data stores to be identified as the project proceeds. The method has mechanisms for including them but be warned, the cost of investigating late arrivals and reprogramming for them rises dramatically as the project progresses. Try to drive out as many as possible as early as possible.

DOCUMENTING LEGACY DATA STORES

Each data source should be documented with at least the following:

- The name of the data store.
- The business area in which it is located.
- The Data Store Owner.
- The Business Domain Expert.
- Where the Legacy Data Store is physically located.

Anecdote

Never underestimate the importance of knowing where a store is located and the obstacles to accessing it when you need it. I have not been caught out yet, but I have come mighty close to finding that a particular user-developed application was not available because the user in question was about to go on maternity leave and the application was on her laptop. Fortunately she had the good sense to warn me. I suppose this illustrates the signal importance of building the virtual team. On the other hand, it might have been better if I had asked when each member of the team expected to be on leave.

- Other data stakeholders as appropriate.
- The format (eg Oracle, Access, Excel).
- The Key Business Data Area(s) the data store covers.
- The entities within the Key Business Area(s) the data store covers.
- Data volumes – both as an absolute count of records by table type and by entity.

> **Hint**
>
> In the case of those entities central to the data migration project, we may need our volumes to go down to a level below each table. In our worked example we may, for instance, only want to migrate Worker records where the company currently employs the person concerned. We are not interested in historical records of past employees.

- Data churn or turnover – is this a volatile data store with large numbers of inputs, amendments and deletions or is this a relatively static data store (see Chapter 7 for a more detailed description)?
- An impressionistic view of data quality, including conformance with the Key Business Data Area model, internal consistency and perceived degree of proximity to the reality it is trying to capture. This must be the view of the Business Domain Experts or possibly the local Technical Data Expert. If the local feeling is that the data is useful then it probably is. You will have the opportunity to test this hypothesis later.
- Ultimately the full field-by-field analysis will be required. This is not needed where the data store is going to be excluded at the first pass. In which case the reason for exclusion should be added.

> **Hint**
>
> A good technique that I have seen used when documenting data quality is to give each Legacy Data Store a two-part score in the range of A1 to D4. The letter relates to the confidence that the data is reliably linked to data in the real world and the number relates to the internal and external consistency of the data. Hence this could be:
>
> A = data gathered by full audit, or from real-time systems;
>
> B = data gathered by statistically valid partial audit or reliably translated from systems gathered to grade A;

C = data gathered from secondary systems or summarized from data gathered to grade B;

D = impressionistic data gathered from limited survey or generated internally from a synthesis of information gathered to grade C.

1 = data measured to within 98% accuracy of the Data Quality Rules;

2 = data measured to within 95% accuracy of the Data Quality Rules;

3 = data measured to within 85% accuracy of the Data Quality Rules;

4 = data less than 85% accurate according to the Data Quality Rules.

Certain grade combinations are not allowed, like A4, because it should not be possible for a full audit to produce less than 85% accuracy.

The benefit of this measure is that it allows different Legacy Data Stores to be valued on a similar basis and hence is increasingly used by government regulators. It is not possible within this document to set firm limits to the values in the ranges. Different industries and systems will have different standards. Just remember Golden Rule 2 and work through the issues with your business population.

- Who uses the data store, what they use it for and how significant it is.

It need not take long to initially document data stores. Create a standard form. Small spreadsheets can be analysed in minutes. Larger data stores obviously require greater analysis. The Legacy Data Store definition should be signed off by the Data Store Owner and filed with the data migration project documentation. The set of Legacy Data Store definitions is one of the key configurable items within the migration process. After the initial free-for-all, new Legacy Data Stores that appear must be change-controlled onto the project. The later they are discovered, the greater the impact in terms of time and cost that they will have. It is imperative that the programme and the user population are made aware of the cost of late disclosure.

Hint

I use any means possible, including posters and email shots, so that everyone is aware of the potential impact of late disclosure of Legacy Data Stores. When they

> come to light (as indeed they invariably do), use the
> programme's change control procedure to get them
> included in the remit of the data migration project. Be
> realistic in your impact assessment, these things can
> really trip you up!

System Retirement Policy

System Retirement Policies

A System Retirement Policy is the specification and plan
for how a Legacy Data Store will be decommissioned.

For each Legacy Data Store we are going to migrate, there should be a
System Retirement Policy. As the definition suggests, a System Retirement
Policy is the place where all the system closedown information is stored. It
is the reassurance to the Data Store Owner that all their concerns will be
addressed in the migration process. Over the course of the project it is built
up until it contains a description, in business English, of what is going to
be migrated and what is not going to be migrated. Where data is not going
to be migrated, but is needed for future enterprise purposes (typically this
is historical transaction data that must be kept for occasional reporting,
audit or regulatory purposes) then the System Retirement Policy will
define where the data will be kept. It also contains details of how systems
will be decommissioned, both the timing (so many days or weeks after go
live) and the manner of decommissioning. This is especially important for
local Legacy Data Stores that can persist in a half-life long after they are
ostensibly replaced by the new system, with their data diverging
increasingly from the new system.

Further reassurance is provided to the Data Store Owner and other key
Data Stakeholders by the data quality checks that are applied before and
after migration. The principal mechanism for controlling data quality – the
Data Quality Rules – are described in detail in Chapter 5 and will exist in
separate documents. However, there are also activities that occur as part of
the migration procedure and these should be recorded in the System
Retirement Policies.

We should negotiate to provide whatever reassurance we can to the Data
Store Owner that their valued data has been transferred accurately. Our
role as Data Migration Analysts is to facilitate the reconciliation between
Golden Rules 1, 2 and 3. We also have to take cognizance of the budgetary
and physical limitations of the larger programme.

The traditional deliverables for checking the reliability of any file transfer
activity are Control Totals, audit trails and user acceptance tests.

Audit trails

> **Audit trail**
> An audit trail is a record of the actions carried out on the data as it progresses through extract, transformation and loading.

In a data migration project, some records just do not make it to the destination. Because of our Data Quality Rules activities (see Chapter 5) we will know in advance how many records will fail. However, it is reassuring to the Data Store Owner to have this tracked. It may also be a legal or regulatory requirement; therefore, make sure that you have identified the appropriate Data Stakeholders to consult for each Legacy Data Store.

Audit trails can be anything from a record of Control Totals (see below for definition of Control Totals) to a back-up store of all the records at each stage of their progression through the migration process. Certainly within the definition of audit trails we should say what we are going to do with records that fail validation at any point. However, as you are negotiating audit trails with your Data Store Owner and Business Domain Expert you may have to remind them of Golden Rule 3. They must understand the cost and benefit of iterating round the load, rejection, fix, reload cycle. But in the end Golden Rules 1 and 2 must be applied. Fortunately once you have read this book and applied its principles you will be having an adult, peer-to-peer conversation.

Audit trails are also used as part of Fallback design (see paragraphs on Fallback design in Chapter 7).

Control Totals

> **Control Total**
> A Control Total is either the sum of some meaningful value within the data being transferred or a count of the number of records being transferred.

For data migration, Control Totals are normally restricted to a count of records rather than adding up the values in a particular field. The count will be performed once in the Legacy Data Store then again in the new system. The two values should be the same, less, of course, the records accounted for in the audit trail.

> **Hint**
>
> This is not always so straightforward. As we will see when we look at Data Mapping (in Chapter 6), one record in the Legacy Data Store may become many in the new system or vice versa. The calculation then becomes trickier. Work with your Data Store Owner and Business Domain expert to devise a set of Control Totals that make sense both from a technical as well as an enterprise viewpoint.

User acceptance tests

In a programme of any size it is normal for there to be a test team. They have all the expertise to define the various levels of testing. Books larger than this one have been devoted to the arcane practices of the system tester. I do not intend to duplicate their content here. Suffice to say that for our purposes we need to get agreement from the Data Stakeholders as to the degree of testing they will want to carry out, in addition to the Control Totals and audit trails that will satisfy them that the data is loaded as they require. These requirements should be expressed in business language. When we look at a model project later (in Part Two) we will see that there is a place where these requirements are fed into the testing team. Of course if you are without a testing team then this is where you will specify what tests you will carry out.

> **Hint**
>
> The testing mix can be quite complicated and is beyond the scope of this book. Testing needs to be carried out on the functionality that the new system is implementing as well as on the data that was transferred, ideally in one suite of tests. Non-functional aspects of the new system (run times, response times etc) also need to be tested. It is influenced by the form of migration (see the section on Data Migration Implementation Forms in Chapter 7) and the varying degrees of safety and mission-criticality of the operations being automated.

The most common form of testing that a Business Domain Expert will want to perform for reassurance is also the least scientific but often the most effective. It is the 'touch and feel' test. Selected users are allowed access to the new system after data load, but before the rest of the user community is allowed on to run their eyes over the screens, and report any anomalies they can find. That the Business Domain Experts will do this anyway whether you formally sanction it or not, you can be assured of. So make it part of your System Retirement Policy as a user acceptance test. Have them (or a user selected representative) on site on the night to perform a final sanity check of touch and feel. It further reinforces their sense of being part of the team.

Hint

I suggest elsewhere in this book, but it bears repeating: make your data migration project as good an experience as possible for all the participants. Involving your Business Domain Experts at go live is a good way of furthering that team building on which your success has depended. You may not experience any benefit from it directly if, like me, you move off immediately to other projects, but it sure helps the next guy down the pike. And we all enjoy a moment of celebration.

Creating System Retirement Policies

Work on System Retirement Policies commences as soon as a Data Store Owner for a Legacy Data Store is identified and the Legacy Data Store is deemed to be one likely to be used for migration purposes. Opening discussions with the key Data Stakeholders about what needs to be done prior to a Legacy Data Store being decommissioned is key to getting user buy-in. As our definition of a Data Store Owner is the person who can commit to turning a system off, it reinforces the message that they own the data migration process and the products of that process.

Hint

I know that this is not original to me but it's worth passing on in any case – it is far easier to get lots of small sign-offs rather than one big one. Get your Data Store Owner used to signing things off at each stage and the last system closedown certificate sign-off will be that much easier. Load one big document on them at the end of the data migration project and you'll find it all the harder.

System Retirement Policies are added to and signed off at each stage of the project until they are signed off as part of the final data migration plan.

Stage 1 data cleansing System Retirement Policies will be signed off with at least the following items covered:

- Outline description of the Legacy Data Store (this can be lifted from the Legacy Data Store definition forms).

- Data retention requirements. These are important when we come to consider how much historical data to migrate. Some systems – for instance your company's financial records – may have a statutory requirement to be retained for a given number of years. We need to know this when we come to data migration design.

- Quantifying access requirements to legacy data. Some data need only be held 'just in case'; other data may need to be available online 24 hours a day, 7 days a week. This information will be used during Data Migration Design.

- Identifying those aspects of a Legacy Data Store that will not be replaced by the new system, for instance where these form part of a completely different Key Business Data Area that is not part of the new system, which may be possible at this stage. Document these because they may disclose the need for the development of legacy system repositories that will persist after new system implementation.

What we are after in the Stage 1 Data Preparation document is a statement of the conditions that must be met prior to the Legacy Data Store being deleted.

> **Hint**
>
> This is similar to a technique high-pressure salesmen use for objection handling. Instead of fearing objections, get them out of the client early. Ask, in effect, 'What conditions do I have to satisfy for you to allow me to switch this system off?' Getting these concerns out in the open early has a number of advantages.
>
> - It starts to build the crucial relationship with the Data Store Owner.
> - It gives everyone time to find solutions.
> - It gives the Data Store Owner time to get used to the fact that the system is going to disappear.
> - It creates an implicit acceptance that if we satisfy all these conditions there is no reason why the final stage System Retirement Policy, committing the system to oblivion, should not be signed.
>
> All too often the first time the Data Store Owner is asked to sign anything is when system closedown is imminent. They are given little time to consult and the natural reaction is to resist being bounced into a decision.

The next stage of data preparation will develop the above further when the Legacy Data Store models are compared with the new system design model. We will then know for certain which Legacy Data Stores will be replaced completely and which will need some way of retaining legacy data that cannot be accommodated in the new system but is still needed.

We will also know, by comparison with their peers, the data stores that should be removed from use as intrinsically unsound duplicates of better quality data elsewhere. We will also know for certain which Legacy Data Stores will remain untouched by the programme.

In the final stage of data migration the System Retirement Policies are completed with what amounts to the business specification from which technical specifications for coding the data migration software and legacy system repositories will be developed. Data Transitional Rules (see below) will be added at this point to cover the interim between the new system being fully live and the Legacy Data Store being run down.

Sign-off at this stage is the death certificate for a Legacy Data Store. By taking the Data Store Owner through, and having them own, the development of the system retirement plans this final sign-off is as painless as possible. But be ruthless. Cull those systems!

Anecdote

All too often this aspect of data migration is overlooked and phantom systems persist in a ghostly half-life, like the undead of some horror movie, causing problems downstream with duplicated data and confusion as to where the 'real' data lies. Pretty soon the enterprise is back in the same mess it started from. If a data store is to be superseded, make sure it is properly killed off!

Data Transitional Rules

Data Transitional Rules

Data Transitional Rules are the temporary business operating procedures put in place to cope with the disturbance caused by data migration itself.

Most business data these days is captured either in real time, as it happens, or shortly afterwards. This means that business transactions are typically recorded piece by piece and rarely as a complete whole. In the 24/7 environment in which most modern business operates it is also not always possible to find an operating window where we can close off core business systems to users whilst we carry out our migration exercises. So if you add together business transactions that span several days or weeks with a 24/7 operating environment and throw in a data migration, then we have to anticipate that there will be overhanging activities that will need to be managed by the business. Obvious examples are in order processing applications. Orders raised in one system will still be being enacted after that Legacy Data Store has been turned off. Data Transitional Rules cover the interim period while some data is not available, in its most up-to-date form. They may require data to be updated in two places at once, or refer the users to some alternative data store for certain items.

Data Transitional Rules are used in System Retirement Policies and in the operating policies for Transient Data Stores amongst other places.

Transient Data Store

Transient Data Stores are temporary databases that are created during the process of data migration. They are needed for a variety of reasons, but should not be allowed to persist beyond the lifetime of the data migration project. They can be as sophisticated as a fully normalized enterprise-strength database or as simple as a spreadsheet.

Data Transitional Rules should not last for more than the duration of the data migration project. As discussed above, System Retirement Polices often expose the need for ongoing maintenance of historic legacy data. If these requirements are to persist beyond project closedown then these rules should be added to the system operating policies of the new system. An example of such a rule is that all orders completed prior to date X should be looked for in the legacy repository, and all orders completed later than that date should be sought in the new system. There would be an ongoing need to brief this rule out when training new staff beyond the end of the project, so this is not a Data Transitional Rule.

Data freeze

Data freeze

The prevention of updates to records after they have been extracted for data migration and before they are loaded into the new system.

Data freezes are really just one type of Data Transitional Rule. They can be useful for some data sets that are migrated early in the data migration timetable – typically the code table type entities – but they do have to be rigorously enforced. A partial data freeze is more common, where only absolutely essential changes are made.

Hint

This is where obeying Golden Rule 1 pays dividends. These rules including data freezes are not imposed from the outside but originate from the enterprise itself.

Chapter review

In this chapter you were introduced to:
- *Key Business Data Areas;*
- *Legacy Data Stores;*
- *System Retirement Policies;*
- *Data Transitional Rules.*

These are key tools in the building of a workable data migration strategy consistent with the Golden Rules.

5 Data Quality Rules

In this chapter you will be introduced to that key tool – the Data Quality Rule. You will be shown:

- *how to construct them;*
- *how to use them;*
- *where to use them;*
- *what a well-constructed Data Quality Rule looks like.*

INTRODUCING DATA QUALITY RULES

Data Quality Rules are central to this method.

- They keep ownership firmly in the hands of the business (Golden Rule 1).
- They expose to the project the knowledge hidden in the business (Golden Rule 2).
- The process of deriving them gets the business to address the issue of the limitations of time and resources (Golden Rule 3).
- They form the contract between the business and the technicians as to what constitutes quality data and how to go about securing it (Golden Rule 4).

On a well-run data migration project you will spend far more time, effort and resource on Data Quality Rules than on any other activity.

So what are Data Quality Rules?

> **Data Quality Rules**
>
> Data Quality Rules are a statement of the metrics that will be used to measure the quality of the data for each of the data sets under consideration, either at Legacy Data Store or Key Business Data Area level, and the set of steps that will bring current data to the level where these metrics are met.

Hint

If I were to be pedantic I would define the Data Quality Rules as 'the statement of metrics that will be used to measure the quality of the data sets under consideration'. As you will see in the paragraphs on what Data Quality Rules documents should contain, there is a 'Method Statements' section for the 'set of steps that will bring current data to the level where these metrics are met'. However, by referring to the whole document as the 'Data Quality Rule' I reinforce in the Stakeholders' minds that a quality statement is not complete without a metric and a method (or mitigation). I then go one step further and shorten Data Quality Rule to DQR. Although this is one of those dreaded Three Letter Acronyms (TLAs), it has the benefit of not having to be changed to make it plural.

Make 'DQR' part of the vocabulary of your data migration project. You will then not have Data Stakeholders presenting you with 'data problems'. They will be requesting additional DQR and so will have accepted the necessity to create metrics and method statements, schedule resources etc. They will have become part of the solution.

They are used at a number of points in a data migration project.

They are used in the first stage of data preparation, where they form the basis of subsequent data cleansing and data preparation activities.

A second set are developed later in data preparation when the new system data design is included and the data prepared in Stage 1 is further enhanced to meet the criteria of the new system.

How Are Data Quality Rules Created?

The most successful way of generating a Data Quality Rule is to invite the Data Stakeholders to a series of facilitated meetings and thrash out the detail face to face (see 'Generating Data Quality Rules' on page 71).

Hint

It is also possible to use the emerging data profiling tools to seek out possible data quality issues. However, keep Golden Rules 1 and 2 in mind. Although this is a good way of creating a 'straw man' to present to your key Data Stakeholders, do not presume that this can tell you the full story.

Use of corporate data models to form baseline

If you are fortunate enough to have the assistance of a Corporate Data Architect, you can use their data models and modelling expertise as the baseline from which to analyse the divergence of Legacy Data Stores that will form the starting point for Data Quality Rules. However, do not discount Legacy Data Stores that do not conform to the corporate model, but use the information sensitively in your Data Quality Rules workshops.

> ### Hint
>
> A key aspect to remember in conversations with the information resource function is that we need to know which data model is being presented to us. This book recommends a two-pass approach to data preparation. In the first we align/measure the difference between the Legacy Data Stores and the legacy data model. In the second we align the legacy data model to the new system data model. Often, the corporate data modellers will have already made this cognitive leap before we arrive on the project and have to be pulled back from an over-enthusiastic, premature rush into moulding legacy data into the new data structure shape.

Data Quality Rules and Legacy Data Stores

It is possible for one Data Quality Rule to address more than one data store and it is possible for a data store to have many Data Quality Rules written for it. However, it is not possible for a Data Quality Rule to address no data stores. Even where the rule is written for a pure data gathering exercise, say to fill a data gap between the Legacy Data Stores and the new system, there will still be a Transient Data Store in the middle to hold new data prior to transmission. Possibly the new system itself may be the data store if the missing data is to be keyed straight in.

First-cut Data Quality Rules

First-cut Data Quality Rules are designed to provide reassurance that legacy data is internally consistent. There is no mapping to the new system, but legacy data is audited to ensure that it will be fit for loading. Any known problems that would inhibit data loading are resolved.

The quality of the Legacy Data Stores, and how rigorously corporate data management techniques have been applied, will partially determine the amount of remedial work that needs to be done. With high quality, well maintained Legacy Data Stores this phase can be restricted to a simple audit, but due diligence dictates that at least one Data Quality Rule be raised so that what is meant by 'quality data' can be rigorously defined and tested. Reassurance that there are no data quality issues is cheaper than uncovering data quality issues once the migration code has been written and time is running short.

Anecdote

Whenever I get involved with 'failing' migration projects I nearly always find that first-cut Data Quality Rules were skimped or are missing altogether. The temptation to trust the corporate Legacy Data Stores is great: after all, these are systems that have been running the company. There are also the issues discussed above of the distance Data Store Owners may have from the day-to-day operation of corporate systems. Resist the temptation to skimp. If nothing else, see it as a dry run for the more complex second-cut Data Quality Rules and use it to build the virtual team you will need to complete the task. However, I guarantee that out of the woodwork data deficiencies will appear that existing work-arounds have covered up.

A more common situation is to be confronted with a mixed bag of systems, of varying quality, which may or may not conform to any corporate standard. Within this disparate bunch of systems there will often be local inconsistencies. It is not uncommon for major corporations to rely, unwittingly, on locally derived data stores, created within the user community, often in spreadsheet format. They may be incompatible with any known corporate standard.

Anecdote

Try to avoid the 'King Canute' mentality to unofficial data stores. I have worked in more than one migration where the official policy of only using the designated corporate systems has led to better quality local data stores being deliberately overlooked. This led to poorer quality data being migrated, user dissatisfaction and the absolute certainty in my mind that those unofficial Legacy Data Stores would be up and running again within days of the new system going live. Once again it is an example of the wrong Data Stakeholders driving the process.

In the first-cut Data Quality Rules we emphasize metrics gathering and creating local consistency. We need to be able to answer the question of what is meant by suitable data quality in a manner that accords with Golden Rules 3 and 4. We need to update the Legacy Data Store definition forms with statements of quality that are backed by clear measurements. Where the data sets fall short of a Data Quality Rule, we need the Data Stakeholders to define either the steps that will get the data measurably to the standard of the rule or to reduce the threshold of acceptance or to drop the rule altogether.

Second-cut Data Quality Rules

It is through the second-cut Data Quality Rules that the new systems data structures are introduced, based on the known data quality of the first-cut Data Quality Rules. The Key Business Data Area will have been brought to a standard level of quality via the first-cut Data Quality Rules, the second-cut Data Quality Rules will take these standardized data sets and derive the rules that will allow them to be mapped onto the new system's requirements. This is more than a data mapping exercise, although a set of extract, transform and load definitions will be delivered as an output. This step works through, with the business, the issues of where, from amongst multiple choices, the most appropriate data source for each data item is. We decide how data structures can be amended to the satisfaction of Data Store Owners to fit the new requirement. Finally we agree how data, possibly never previously gathered but necessary for the new system, can be generated. This is the application of the new system data requirements to the knowledge we now have of legacy data stores and the creation of steps that will get us from the old to the new. The whole process is led and owned by the business areas affected.

Iteration

For both first and second-cut Data Quality Rules there may be more than one iteration through the Data Quality Rules process. Typically in first-cut Data Quality Rules the first iteration is one of establishing a baseline of rules and measuring the Legacy Data Stores against those rules. The second iteration takes the findings of the first and records data cleansing activities to solve the issues uncovered.

> **Hint**
>
> Although Data Quality Rules are iterative, with one Data Quality Rule revealing issues that can only be dealt with by another Data Quality Rule, multiple Data Quality Rules iterations are to be avoided. Better quality products in the earlier stages of this method are key to reducing the number of cycles. The better the identification and initial analysis of the Legacy Data Stores, the fewer additional data stores will emerge downstream. The better the identification of Data Stakeholders is carried out, the better the business knowledge that is shared, which in turn reduces the number of data quality surprises.

Types of Data Quality Rules

There are different types of Data Quality Rules and therefore different types of possible data migration failure:

- **Internal consistency:** The commonest type of rule drawn up by technicians for data loading. This covers all the standard data load validation criteria – range checking, data type checking, referential integrity checking, reasonableness checking etc. These check one Legacy Data Store against its own rules.

- **External consistency:** This extends internal consistency checks of a Legacy Data Store with the wider system environment. It checks the Legacy Data Stores against the Key Business Data Area rules in first-cut Data Quality Rules and against the new system requirements in second-cut Data Quality Rules.

- **Reality Check:** This is the sort of checking that typically technicians do not attempt because the answers lie outside of the data held in computer systems, in the reality of the business world. But it is an issue that the project must address because it is an issue that causes friction between the business and the project when a new system starts to run either for real, or in parallel. Just because all the internal consistency rules are met does not mean that the data item corresponds with a genuine piece of business reality. It reinforces the need to keep Golden Rule 1 at the forefront of any migration project.

a

Anecdote

I have seen migration data sets where whole hotels have been duplicated, or where lengths of pipeline that I can see out of the window of the office do not exist in the appropriate data set. Often the Reality Check data error hints at the existence of a data set we have yet to uncover – otherwise how did the business previously function? Asking this question often drives out the missing data set. When it does, invoke the change control procedure, create a new Legacy Data Store definition form, and bring the new system into consideration.

I prefer a two-pass approach like this because:

Out of the first-cut Data Quality Rules we get a range of Key Business Data Areas that contain Legacy Data Stores that, to a known degree, are internally consistent, consistent with the model of the Key Business Data Area and correspond with the real world.

In the second-cut Data Quality Rules we introduce the data model of the new system. We can now approach the question of how we migrate from the Legacy Data Store to the new system confident that we are basing our judgements on known data qualities (and weaknesses – remember Golden Rule 3).

A TYPICAL DATA QUALITY RULE DOCUMENT

I am aware that each company, and each project within each company, will have their own documentation standards. What I illustrate here are the minimum items that should be in a Data Quality Rules document for it to be effective.

Introduction

Not everyone who picks up this document will know what a Data Quality Rule is for. Explain briefly the purpose of the document within your project. Explain the process taken to generate the document. A standard paragraph is often enough. If you are bulking up Data Quality Rules into a single package (possibly all the Data Quality Rules for a single Key Business Data Area) then this section can be omitted from each individual Data Quality Rule and a general introduction for the package may suffice.

Scope

Define the limits of this Data Quality Rule. Is it for the whole of a Key Business Data Area or for a single aspect of a single Legacy Data Store? Is it an investigation into data quality that will subsequently be used as the metrics of a later Data Quality Rule or is it a second-pass Data Quality Rule that will prepare the data for migration?

Personnel

In the Personnel section of a Data Quality Rule we list those who contributed either directly or by proxy in the creation of this Data Quality Rule. I find it useful to have a standard tabular format with name, official job title, Data Stakeholder role, phone number or email address and whether they contributed directly or by proxy. All Data Quality Rules must have the Data Store Owner and Business Domain Expert for the Legacy Data Store(s) involved identified here.

Key Business Data Area or Legacy Data Store

Name the Key Business Data Area(s) or Legacy Data Store that this Data Quality Rules document covers. There should be a brief recap of the chief data items mastered by this Key Business Data Area and/or Legacy Data Store. This may be duplication of what is in previous documents but remember that this document will be read by some people in isolation and should be as stand-alone as possible. Also, where a large data source is concerned, one Data Quality Rules document may only cover part of the data source. So be explicit about what the document covers and what it does not cover out of the chief data items mastered by the data source or business area.

DATA QUALITY ASSESSMENT

First capture the impressionistic opinions of the key Data Stakeholders, then move on to the quantitative assessment that fits Golden Rule 4. The impressionistic assessment can be cut and pasted from the Legacy Data Stores forms.

Qualitative assessment

Include a brief statement of the perceived business value of the data – for instance that this is the primary sales forecasting system for the company or that this system has a regulatory significance.

If this is a first-cut Data Quality Rules document, capture here the perceived internal and external data consistency – the accuracy, the age of the data and its relationship to external reality. If this is a second-cut Data Quality Rules document, record the results of the previous Data Quality Rules documents as appropriate to inform the next section.

This assessment should be available from previous forms and can be cut and pasted into the document. Keep this section brief but remember that not everyone who reads it will have read all the preceding documentation and a Data Quality Rules document should be a stand-alone document. Do not assume that the reader has the knowledge that the project has by now acquired. The qualitative assessment is the springboard to the more useful quantitative assessment, so try to be both brief and accurate.

Quantitative assessment

For each issue identified in the qualitative assessment, either a quantitative statement is required or, where there is no way of realistically measuring the truth value of the qualitative statement, a mitigation can be added.

> ### Anecdote
>
> I was working on a project for a large utility company and there was doubt about the adequacy of some of the very old (Victorian) under-ground asset records. Clearly it was not tenable to dig up the assets to look at them. We had to accept that these records were as good as we were going to get and estimate the data quality based on the limited sample of assets that had been exhumed over the previous two years. Remember Golden Rules 1 and 2 – be led by the business on what is adequate and realistic.

By and large, though, we are trying to follow Golden Rule 4. To retain control the project needs to know what set of steps we are going to carry out and how we are to measure our success. The quantitative statement should record the number of key data items (eg 200 sites or 3,000 suppliers) and any known internal, external or Reality Check errors or suspicions.

Each quantitative statement must be accompanied by a testable verification rule (eg run a query to check that each supplier code on the purchasing system matches an account code in goods receivable). Remember that we will be recording both known errors and known strengths. Check both.

METHOD STATEMENTS

A method statement is required whenever a Data Quality Rule is suggested. This will show how far the source data fulfils the Data Quality Rules requirement. Where the source data fails to meet a Data Quality Rules standard a further method statement will be required either to explain what is to be done about the data or to explain what mitigation is going to take place to accommodate less than perfect data.

Data cleansing method statements

A data cleansing method statement must include the following parts:

- the physical data elements involved;
- an unequivocal statement of the rule in a format that can be measured;
- how the current data matches up to the rule (output from the Data Quality Rules statement);
- the steps that will be taken to get the data from its present state to the desired state;
- who will carry out which steps (real names, with completion dates etc);
- what measure will be used to gauge that each step has been completed.

Data cleansing method statements must be developed jointly with the business. Even if it is tempting to just go and fix something, do not succumb to the temptation. The business must own not just the data but also the quality of the data. The business must own the steps that get from the current state of the data to the desired state. This does not mean that you cannot heavily suggest a certain course of action, but it must be endorsed and owned by the business.

Although the method statement will specify where the data cleansing will take place (eg in a specially constructed Transitional Data Store or in the original data store) and how in general the cleansing will happen (eg line by line on screen or by mass query), data cleansing method statements should be kept as short and pithy as possible. The detailed description of what is to be done occurs in the 'Mitigation tasks' section opposite. The method statement provides a high-level description of how the Data Quality Rules are to be carried out.

Perhaps a Transitional Data Store needs to be built. Although this needs to be specified in detail somewhere, this is not the place for a full description of it. You should be aiming for a statement not exceeding one page of A4 that can be read by all of the Data Stakeholders without losing some of them in the detail. Refer to other business specifications as necessary so that those who need to can follow the description.

> **Hint**
>
> Where an Intermediary Data Store is being used there must be Data Transitional Rules in place to keep the data in the Transitional Data Store in step with a changing business reality. Data Transitional Rules are discussed in Chapter 4.

Mitigation statements

Use mitigation statements where the Data Stakeholders agree that, although they flout a Data Quality Rule, under Golden Rule 3 we do not have the time or the need to further cleanse the records. Mitigation Statements often exclude certain records (eg records before a certain date will be excluded from migration) or place limits on the quality of the final product (eg it is acceptable that business premises below $40m^2$ do not have a designated key holder). It is not the data migration project's responsibility to define these limits, it is the data migration project's responsibility to create a situation where the various Data Stakeholders can achieve a viable compromise between their differing requirements, so that, for instance, the Programme Expert's need for referential integrity constraints to be met is not compromised by the Business Domain Expert's ability to manage without explicit links between some data items.

> **Anecdote**
>
> On many projects on which I have worked the Programme Expert's view of data quality requirements has been allowed to take precedence over the Business Domain Expert's view only to be scuppered by a mystifying lack of co-operation from the business. What I try to achieve is mutual recognition of the two sides' areas of expertise and then create opportunities for the dialogue between them to be creative. If the Programme Expert cannot function without the creation of some link

that is not in the legacy data, an atmosphere of trust and mutual respect is more likely to get the issue resolved speedily.

Mitigation Tasks

Each method statement should be broken down into a series of Tasks. Each Task should conform to the standard project planning view of SMART tasks. They should be Simple, Measurable, Appropriate, Realistic and Timely. Each Task must therefore be of known duration and have known resources that will apply a predicted amount of effort to complete the Task. There must be some measurable quantitative change that the Task makes, agreed in advance and aligned to the Data Quality Rules, against which progress can be tracked.

Hint

One of my criticisms of the usual ad hoc approach to data migration is that it does not contain standardized work packages that allow for the migration activity to be tracked at programme level. Breaking data cleansing, the principal activity, down into methods and tasks allows different levels of control by the programme office. I do not normally recommend that the low level of detail in the Tasks is copied onto the programme plan. Method statements are usually sufficient to form Programme level activities. The duration, resource and effort values for the Tasks can be rolled up to calculate the duration, resource and effort value for the Method. The tasks are monitored within the data migration sub-project and the programme office can be confident that reported completion percentages are accurate reflections of deliverables from lower level Tasks.

Quantitative changes should be tracked openly and shared with the other Stakeholders on an agreed, regular basis. My normal suggestion is fortnightly.

Hint

Although I do not advocate open competition to complete Data Quality Rules, transparent reporting does encourage commitment to the data cleansing activity. Agree in advance the reporting interval and stick to it. I have found that after the second publication of quantitative results peer group pressure ensures that the level of commitment to completing the task increases, especially amongst the less enthusiastic. And remember that if properly derived, these are not tasks imposed from without but ones generated and owned by the business units completing them. Also remember, however, to be supportive. Modern slimmed-down businesses have little spare capacity to handle additional tasks and the day job may have to come first and Golden Rule 3 may have to be considered.

The resources to complete each task will mostly be from the list of Data Stakeholders but may include technical resources where Transitional Data Stores need to be built. If a new resource is identified, other than purely technical, update the stakeholder list on the Legacy Data Store definition form.

Hint

Unlike other projects, a large part of data migration projects' resources will be within the business and outside the direct management control of anyone on the project. Do not expect that tidy timesheets will be returned with the 'Effort' and 'Expected Remaining Duration' columns filled in. The people in the business may be fitting this work in alongside the day job. To provide project controls we therefore rely on measuring the quantitative changes and regular liaison with the virtual team out in the real world. And don't be surprised if the whole task is accomplished in the last few days of the estimated elapsed duration.

METRICS

The metrics are the rest of the world's window into the progress of data preparation. They are the consolidation of the quantitative changes measured in the Data Quality Tasks, presented at a level that informs the programme of the speed of delivery. The metrics will highlight areas of concern for the programme where some essential data cleansing activity is falling behind and provide reassurance that targets will be reached.

Consolidation should be in a form that can be turned into a graph or a chart that can be published.

Hint

Make all the metrics point the same way so that comparisons are easier. I prefer charts where 100% means that the task is complete: 100% complete has a more positive feel than 0% remaining errors!

Anecdote

Keeping metrics can be fun and part of the team building process. In one very large migration where multiple analysts were running multiple Data Quality Rules, we instituted a graphic in the form of a Formula One race track with each Key Business Data Area a separate car. We could then see who was 'winning' in the race to 100% compliance.

GENERATING DATA QUALITY RULES

Data Quality Rules should be created by the Data Stakeholders but facilitated in their production by the data migration project. What I describe below is the ideal environment for creating Data Quality Rules. I am aware that in the real world in which most of us operate this ideal may not be possible; therefore, I also include pointers to possible work-arounds, but we should strive for the perfect situation where possible.

The best Data Quality Rules are created in a single facilitated session, with all the Data Stakeholders with an interest in the domain of the problem present, supported by sufficient technical resources. I will not, here, describe how a well-run, facilitated meeting should operate, there are enough quality books on this subject. But I will show how that kind of forum is best suited to creating Data Quality Rules.

Settings for a Data Quality Rules meeting

For the optimum creation of Data Quality Rules a dedicated meeting room is required. The room should be big enough to seat all the delegates, with space for break-out sessions where these might be useful. The room should be stocked with all the normal meeting room equipment – whiteboard, flip charts, overhead projector, pens, pencils, paper etc.

Hint

Ban the use of mobile phones and pagers and remove all desk phones from the meeting place.

As a minimum, report access to the Legacy Data Stores being considered, at least at reporting level, is extremely useful, as is access to the migration tool of choice and to software suitable for building prototypes of Transitional Data Stores (I normally rely on Microsoft Access).

> **Hint**
>
> Make the sessions as hospitable as possible. Providing lunch is a great way to mingle with and get the real views of the delegates, and it also provides an opportunity for the technical team to create prototypes and/or reports to perform an initial check on emerging Data Quality Rules. This is also the time to build the virtual team essential to completing the task.

Personnel

The following Data Stakeholders are compulsory.

- Data Store Owner (or delegate with authority to make decisions on their behalf);
- Business Domain Experts;
- Data Migration Analysts.

The following Data Stakeholders may be necessary:

- Data Customers;
- regulatory representatives;
- Programme Experts (for second-cut Data Quality Rules).

In addition the data migration team should provide:

- a facilitator;
- a scribe;
- a data analyst/programmer (optional but useful).

In advance of the meeting

Explain the purpose of the meeting, what the Key Business Data Area is and which Legacy Data Stores within the Key Business Data Area will be discussed.

> **Hint**
>
> I often prepare a 'straw man' Data Quality Rule to introduce the Data Stakeholders to the concepts involved and the kinds of outputs expected of them. There is a risk here, though – you have to make sure that everyone who reads it knows that it is not the real thing.

For first-cut Data Quality Rules:

- Read through the Legacy Data Stores definition forms. These will give some initial ideas of the qualitative data issues, around which the meeting can be structured.
- Data issues with legacy data are often well known – ask around.
- Compare the data model for the Legacy Data Store and the Business Data Area looking for structural problems.
- If this is a first-pass Data Quality Rule assess how far the Legacy Data Store obeys its own data model constraints. This is where automated tools are useful.

For second-cut Data Quality Rules:

- Compare the Key Business Data Area data model and the new system data model looking for structural problems.
- Compare the Legacy Data Stores and the new system data requirements documentation to uncover the detailed mapping issues.
- Compare the Legacy Data Stores definition forms to find where alternative data for migration may be located.
- Re-read the first-cut Data Quality Rules and the Legacy Data Stores definition forms.

From these sources data issues will be apparent, but it is important to network as widely as possible to uncover the issues that need to be addressed.

Chapter review

In this chapter you were introduced to Data Quality Rules.
You were also introduced to my preference for adopting a two-pass approach to data migration.

6 Data Gaps and Data Mapping

This chapter introduces the standard features of data migration projects and shows how to apply the concepts outlined previously to them. It covers:

- *data structure comparison;*
- *data gaps;*
- *Data Mapping tables;*
- *data validation;*
- *data selection;*
- *data navigation;*
- *data source to data destination ratios.*

HEALTH WARNING

If you are an experienced IT practitioner, you probably (rightly) feel that you do not need a refresher on these topics. However, I advise you to read over this chapter all the same, because I will be relating the techniques I introduced in the early chapters to the problems with which you are familiar.

Also, as you will be aware, there are many dialects in IT and it helps with the rest of the book if we agree on the meaning of some of the terms we are using.

Hint

The less experienced should also be aware that there are synonyms for most terms in IT. Almost every definition I use in this book (aside from the ones I coined myself) will be challenged by someone who has a penchant for using a different vocabulary. If you encounter a variant do not be afraid to ask for an explanation and try, as I try, not to be too precious about one label or another. It is more important that the project as a whole uses the same terminology than embarking on a spurious search for the 'correct' set.

For the less experienced this is a guided tour over the commonly accepted terms and techniques of data migration exercises. You will emerge better equipped to deal on level terms with other technical experts you meet. This section does contain some fairly esoteric descriptions of the application of data modelling techniques. If you are reading this book as a manager or purchaser of data migration consultancy, feel free to glaze over when the going gets too tough. I would still advise you to read it though, because it contains descriptions of common migration problems and suggested solutions.

STANDARD DATA MIGRATION TERMS

First let us cover the basics by agreeing some terms. For those of you new to data migration it will be illuminating, for those longer in the tooth it will allow us to agree a set of definitions going forward.

Selection

Often we do not want to migrate all the historical data from the Legacy Data Stores to the new system data stores. Perhaps, in our worked example, we only want Work Rosters that have been carried out in the last two years, and Equipment records for equipment that is in use, mothballed or on standby. Therefore we need to be able to select on Date and Equipment Status. Selection will be driven by the requirements of the System Retirement Policies. This is the mechanism that allows the key Data Stakeholders – Data Store Owners, Business Domain Experts, Audit and Regulatory Experts, Programme Experts, Technical Data Experts – to come together to inform the project of the needs of the business going forward.

Navigation

In anything other than a simple data migration we often have to derive data values from more than one table or even more than one Legacy Data Store. We need rules to 'navigate' from one Legacy Data Store to another. This is an area where the technicians often feel the most comfortable, but beware, it is the data that the key Data Stakeholder consensus suggests is the most important that we should go for, not the data that the Technical Data Experts are satisfied with. These are sometimes not the same. We have to balance the advice of the Technical Data Experts and the Programme Experts against the knowledge of the Business Domain Experts.

> **Hint**
>
> Be careful about the charms of a useful extract or load tool. These can be limited in their ability to access data that is held in some of the more unorthodox Legacy Data Stores. IT professionals also have a preference for data stores built according to the rules of good software design – and this excludes most end-user created Legacy Data Stores. We are after the best and most appropriate data, however ill-shaped its setting.

If in doubt, run a Data Quality Rules workshop to get an objective measure as to the most appropriate data source.

Below we will go through worked examples of several different types of navigation as we set out to build the Equipment table's Data Mapping rules.

Validation

Any programmer worth their salt will know that we never blindly enter data into a new system. We scrupulously check it for obvious errors. These include:

- **Range:** Checks that the data item is within a sensible range of values (eg no employee will have a date of birth that would make them less than 16 years old or greater than 75 years old).
- **Mandatory value:** Makes it impossible to create an entry in the table without this field being filled (also known as 'presence' check).
- **Length:** Checks that the data item is the length we expect (eg an Equipment Model Number must not be longer than 20 characters).
- **Data type:** Checks that the data item is of the expected data type (eg Equipment Run Time must be numeric).
- **Data profile:** Checks that the data item is of the expected format (eg zip code or postcode format).
- **Referential integrity:** Checks that the data is consistent with data elsewhere in the system (eg does the Employee Absence Code match a valid code on the Absence Reason table).

However, beware: these checks only tell us that the data is as we expect it. It does not tell us that it is correct – in other words, that it matches something in the real world. For these Reality Checks you need to work with your key Data Stakeholders to produce Data Quality Rules to produce Reality Checks on those items that are significant to the Data Stakeholders. Always keep Golden Rules 2 and 3 in mind, of course. You will never have the time or resources to check every item against existent reality, even if that were theoretically possible. Run your Data Quality Rules workshops to establish where best to direct your effort. Create and work through the Data Quality Rules and the result will be a known level of confidence in the reality of your data whatever its data type or referential integrity constraints are.

DATA GAP ANALYSIS

As I indicated earlier, I am a devotee of data modelling when it comes to data migration. What I present here are some (reasonably) simple examples of how to use data models to spot data gaps and how to use data models to help bridge them.

Data gap analysis should be a first-order task before the detailed Data Mapping occurs. As we shall see, it informs our selection and navigation rules. By taking the 'helicopter view' that data modelling provides we can confront gaps in the legacy data early. And the earlier we confront them, the better. There are, however, limitations to data modelling:

- It can only verify that the structure is correct, it cannot perform a Reality Check.

- It cannot necessarily reveal that look-up data matches (eg that the legacy Equipment Item Types match directly the new system Equipment Types), only that both models have a Type field.

- It cannot reveal anything about whether a table or field is populated (that is, just because the field or table exists, it does not follow that it will have anything in it).

All these will have to be checked via Data Quality Rules or assumed to be correct. Golden Rule 2 very much applies here. Find out from your key Data Stakeholders where activity should be focussed. Items that are missed, or assumptions that prove incorrect will be caught when we get to Data Mapping.

Worked example

The rest of this chapter will use the Equipment conceptual entity and we will see how, by first performing data model comparisons then data gap analysis, we can better inform our Data Mapping and exercise more control over the project.

First let us see what the new system version of this looks like (figure 6.1).

New system Equipment conceptual entity

Please note the following:

- Only the linking entity in a different conceptual entity is shown. We know there are other entities within the different conceptual entity but we omit them for clarity in the diagram.

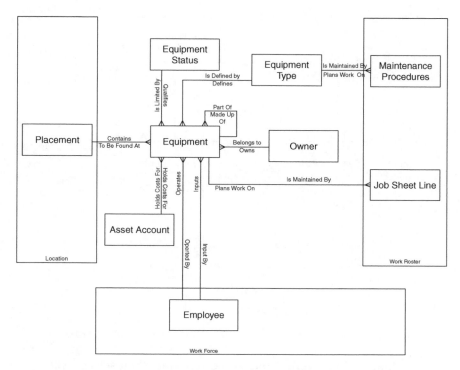

FIGURE 6.1 *New system Equipment entity relationship diagram*

- By taking the model down a level we realize that our original Conceptual Entity Model was incorrect – it did not have any relationships between Work Force and Equipment. We should go back and amend our documentation.

- I have not created an associative entity to resolve the involuted data relationship Equipment has with itself. This is because in the physical implementation there is no such matching table. Each Equipment record holds a pointer to its owner in the hierarchy. The top record holds a null pointer. If there had been a matching table I would have created an associative entity.

Now let us look at the entity relationship diagram from our primary Legacy Data Store – the old Equipment Register. From our library of Legacy Data Store forms we find the diagram in figure 6.2.

Instantly we can see that Owner, Employee, Maintenance Procedures and Job Sheet Line are missing. After a quick discussion within the data migration team, it is agreed that, given the complexity of the new Work Register area, it is sensible for Employee, Maintenance Procedures and Job Sheet Line to be picked up within the Work Force and Work Roster Key Business Data Areas respectively. It is also agreed that the Equipment Key Business Data Area will master the Location (Site) and Employee

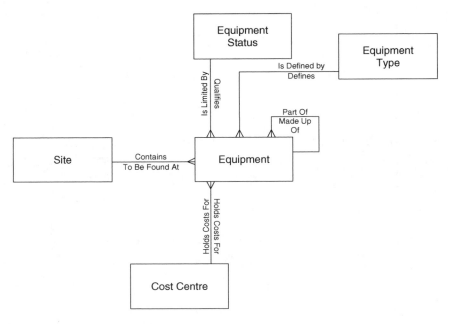

FIGURE 6.2 *Equipment Legacy Data Store*

relationships even though the entities themselves will remain the responsibility of Location and Workforce respectively.

> **Hint**
>
> This illustrates the benefit of clearly breaking up the data migration project by conceptual entity. Where relationships cross the conceptual entity boundary, make one side or the other responsible for it. This makes planning clear-cut. We can see where the inter-team dependencies lie and can plan joint workshops accordingly.

Therefore, as the Equipment Key Business Area, we are left with Owner and the relationships to Employee and Location to manage.

Owner

In the old Equipment Register, equipment that was not the property of our enterprise was either absent or not specially marked. We need to find a way of identifying those Equipment Items that are on loan or lease or even maintained under contract and differentiating them. The answer is to go to the Legacy Data Store catalogue and search for the missing information. We can expect that someone in the enterprise had a need to track items that belong to another company and account for them differently.

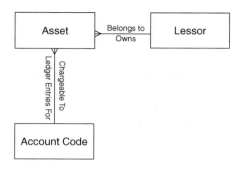

FIGURE 6.3 *Owner Legacy Data Store*

We need to search for Legacy Data Stores that relate to the Equipment conceptual entity. It comes as no surprise to find a spreadsheet in the Accounts department that was used to control the payment to lessors. The data model is illustrated in figure 6.3.

We are not fooled by the different names for the entities and the relationships. After all, different analysts prepared them independently.

> **Hint**
>
> **My mantra on this subject is (although not original to me) 'Names do not define entities, attributes define entities'.**

We check over the Legacy Data Store form and find that the author of the spreadsheet has included the legacy Equipment Item's ID. She used it, apparently, with reference to the Disposals Report to prevent Equipment Items that did not belong to the enterprise being sold off without the lessor's permission.

But is that enough? Well possibly! Remember this is an end user created spreadsheet. We check the Legacy Data Store form and find that it was initially dismissed as being of little use and probably derived from the Equipment Register. It was built for very specific purposes and has been maintained by an enthusiastic and dedicated employee. We need to run a Data Quality Rule against it to see how closely the values in it match the values in the legacy Equipment Item table. We have been told that not all the items maintained by us were recorded in the legacy Equipment Item table. This is then a real find, not only do we have a way of populating a field, we can also enhance the data quality of one of our key tables. Celebrate this success. Make sure it is publicized. You are now not just a cost to the project you are adding value to the enterprise. (I would always contend that guaranteeing appropriate quality data to the enterprise was of value in any case but it does no harm reminding people.)

We upgrade this Legacy Data Store to one that is now a prime candidate for us to use.

Employee

We check our Legacy Data Store library against the Workforce conceptual entity. Although there are plenty of Legacy Data Stores within the Work Force Key Business Data Area that hold information about employees, there are none that hold the relationships we want between Equipment and Employees. This is a data gap we cannot fix using existing data. We record the fact on the issues list and pass the task down to the next level in the data hierarchy – Data Mapping

Before we hand over to Data Mapping

Remember that these techniques will be used at two different times within our project. The examples we have seen relate to the pre-Data Mapping gap analysis, but a similar analysis will be performed between the Key Business Data Areas models and the target Legacy Data Stores. Do not expect that there will be uniformity of design across the Legacy Data Stores. Indeed, expect the opposite.

We will also use parts of the techniques outlined below to understand the navigations and cross Legacy Data Store links we may need to make to create a coherent set of data items that we can say are a full representation of the legacy data set.

DATA MAPPING

This is the core of moving data from one (legacy) system to another (new or target) system. At a field by field level we need to know where each byte of data is coming from, where it is going to and what we need to do to reshape it on the way through.

Data Mapping

A Data Mapping is the rule by which one or more data items in a Legacy Data Store will have their values moved to one or more items in the new system database.

In the overwhelming majority of cases, this involves a one-to-one match of legacy to target. However, as the definition suggests, this may involve splitting a value in one data store into a number of values in the target data store. Conversely it can mean combining more than one value from the Legacy Data Stores into one value in the target data store. The worst case is where multiple values from the Legacy Data store need to be combined then split over multiple values in the target.

Hint

These relationships are usually expressed as a ratio of the form *number of source fields : number of destination fields* so that
- 1:1 means one source field to one destination field;
- 1:M means one source field to many destination fields;
- M:M means many source fields to many destination fields, and so on.

But be wary, nomenclature can vary. Often the letter 'N' is used in place of 'M' (meaning 'a number of'). If in doubt, ask.

Clearly 1:1 mappings need no further transformation rules. They may still have complex selection and navigation rules depending on the data structures we are dealing with. Anything with an M in the relationship, however, will need rules explaining how to split or consolidate values.

Hint

Data Mapping has been joined by the kindred three letter acronym ETL. This stands for extract, transform and load. Strictly speaking, Data Mapping is the task of matching new system (or target) fields to a Legacy Data Store field (or fields). ETL is the software, and therefore the rules, by which data is taken out of one field, validated, manipulated and loaded into another field. There has been an explosion of software products in this area to perform this task. It strikes me that this is a distinction without a difference. But if you are running

> **a data migration project, expect to encounter both terms.**

Worked example

From our data migration example, if we look at the new system Equipment table (as represented in figure 6.1), taking the first 11 fields, we create a table as seen in table 6.1.

We can see the ones that need to be populated (mandatory) from a new system view point. That, however, is only the technical view of mandatory. Although the new system might allow us to create records with some fields unpopulated, our business processes mandate the completion of many other fields. We would also like to provide as rich a data set as possible so in the course of our analysis we have found source data for as many fields as possible.

Looking at it field by field:

Equipment ID: This is a system-generated unique key, so we do not have to provide any values.

Description: It has been agreed that this field will hold the additional information about the condition of the asset and its precise location within a plant. This exists in a matching field in the Asset Inventory Legacy Data Store table, Equipment Item. This is therefore a 1:1 mapping with a simple navigation.

Type: This is trickier. It has been decided that we need to expand the number of types on our new Equipment register from the limited number on the old Equipment Item. This is so that we can apply the correct maintenance routines against them. The old Equipment Item had the allowed values for its Type fields as seen in table 6.2 (in part).

The new system Equipment Types can take more values – at least where pumps are concerned (see table 6.3).

We have a 1:M mapping. That is, one value on the old system can be one of many values on the new. Assuming there is no way of finding the correct new value from other data, then we must appeal to our Business Domain Experts to give us the correct new value. Normally this would be done via a Transitional Data Store. The first step would be to list all the valid old to new combinations in a cross-reference table as shown in table 6.4.

This is not usually a particularly onerous task. The next one, however, when we ask our Business Domain Experts to link existing Equipment Items to the new Equipment Types, can be huge. The Equipment table may contain tens of thousands, even millions, of rows. If you need the enterprise to inspect each record, compare it with what exists in reality and then report back, you may need to allow a substantial amount of time, effort and money in your plan.

TABLE 6.1 *New system Equipment table layout*

Table Name	Field Name	Field Type	Field Length	Mandatory	Description	Validation
				Target		
Equipment	Equipment ID	Integer		Y	Primary Key	Must be unique across the Equipment Table
	Description	Character	200	N	Free Text	None
	Type	Integer		Y	Key of Equipment Type File	Must exist on the Equipment Type File
	Status	Character	2		In Use; Obsolete: Scrapped; On Standby etc	Must exist on the Equipment Status File
	Location ID	Integer		Y	Key Of Location File	Must exist on Location File with Status set to 'Operational', 'Mothballed' or 'Stand By'
	Owner	Character	8	N	Key Of Owner File (some equipment assets are owned by third parties but maintained by us)	Must exist as Owner on Owner File with Status set to 'Current'
	Input By	Character	8	Y	Key of Employee File	Must exist as Employee on Employee File with Status set to 'Employed'
	Operator	Character	8	N	Key of Employee File	Must exist as Employee on Employee File with Status set to 'Employed'
	Warranty Date	Date		N	Date warranty expires (inclusive date)	
	Warranty Description	Character	200	N		Mandatory if Warranty Date Not Null
	Account Code	Integer		Y	Key of the Asset Account File	Must exist on the Asset Account File with a status of 'Active'

TABLE 6.2 *Equipment Item Type table*

Type	Description
HD	Beam lifter
GN	Generator
MC	Macerator
PM	Pump

TABLE 6.3 *Equipment Type table*

Type	Description
3999	Beam lifter
4000	Macerator
4001	High lift pump
4002	Rotory pump
4003	Impellor pump
4004	Oil pump
4005	Generator >10,000 kw
4006	Generator <10,000 kw

TABLE 6.4 *Equipment Type cross-reference table*

Old Type	New Type
HD	3999
GN	4005
GN	4006
MC	4000
PM	4001
PM	4002
PM	4003
PM	4004

This is where an open door policy to Legacy Data Stores and a virtual team of Data Stakeholders are essential. With the help of your Business Domain Experts, go back through the Legacy Data Store catalogue. In our example, although we are getting most of our Equipment information from the legacy Equipment Item table, all this equipment was being maintained prior to the new system being implemented. From the Legacy Data Store sources of the maintenance records we find that the maintenance routines allow us to infer the Equipment Type.

This of course assumes that the Legacy Data Store holding the Maintenance records and the Equipment Item Legacy Data Store have keys in common that allow us to link the two. It also assumes that all records that have a 1:M relationship of legacy Equipment List Type to new system Equipment Type exist in both systems. We need to plan and perform a Data Quality Rule exercise to evaluate this. A second Data Quality Rule may then have to be created to correct any that are missing from one or other Legacy Data Store.

To keep the example simple we find out that the two Legacy Data Stores are a perfect match (unlikely as that may be in reality).

This is a perfect illustration of the need to have performed an adequate analysis of Legacy Data Stores, via first-cut Data Quality Rules workshops, before we get to the mapping issues.

Hint

The worst case is that you may have to review your whole population on a record by record basis. But there are alternatives. Can you get by with a Data Transitional Rule whereby a 'best guess' (in our example case possibly based on Account Code or Location) is applied and an update data sheet goes out on the first maintenance visit? Confer with, and take advice from, your key Data Stakeholders. Make it a business problem. Issues like this often need a wide range of input, not only has the Data Store Owner got to OK the solution, often regulatory and new system imperatives have to be taken into account. Use your virtual team to bring the intelligence and initiative of the whole enterprise to bear. A Data Quality Rule workshop with a Data Transitional Rule written into the appropriate System Retirement Policy will often get around the problem to the satisfaction of all.

The eventual outcome will be a cross-reference table that will be used at data load time to pick up the new Equipment Type from the old Equipment Item ID. This Transient Data Store will have to be created and maintained during the lifetime of the migration project. Although it will be fairly static in this example, there will be some churn in equipment, as new machines replace old ones. A Data Transitional Rule will be created that will make sure that as the, soon to be legacy, Equipment Item table is updated with new rows, the Equipment cross-reference table is also updated with matching rows (see table 6.5)

TABLE 6.5 *Equipment cross-reference table*

Equipment Item ID	New Type	Old Equipment Item Type
SG421	3999	HD
VP563	4003	PM
CX470	4002	PM
JM378	4003	PM
PJ334	3999	HD

Our 1:M example therefore has both a complex mapping and, possibly, a complex navigation.

Equipment Status: Because the enterprise has decided to rationalize the plethora of old Statuses that existed in the Equipment Item table (many now obsolete) Equipment Status is going to be a M:1. A simple Old to New Status table is all that is needed. At data load time, as each Equipment Item is selected, the migration software will go to the cross-reference table and pick up the new code, substituting it in place of the old.

Equipment Location: This presents us with the biggest challenge. Equipment Location corresponds to the Site field in the legacy Equipment Item table but, because the new system is going to be supporting maintenance as well as asset repository information, the new system needs a finer granularity of information. The new system needs to know where, within the bigger sites, the equipment is located. However, over the course of time some of the smaller sites have been amalgamated into larger units. This information has not always been reflected in the Legacy Data Store. So we have a situation where, although some legacy Equipment Item records will be split over more Locations than previously, many Equipment Item records will have their Site fields combined into a single Location. We have a M:M relationship. In report terms this may appear as in table 6.6.

How do we tackle issues like this?

There are a number of practical options available:

TABLE 6.6 *Location cross-reference table*

Legacy Site		New Location		
Description	ID	Description	ID	
Hartleson Depot	HD	Hartleson Depot	3702	Here legacy ID 'GM' maps onto three possible new IDs, but one new ID '3705' maps onto two possible legacy IDs. This is a M:M
Gibb Creek Machine Shop	GM	GCM Floor 1 Bay 1	3703	
Gibb Creek Machine Shop	GM	GCM Floor 1 Bay 2	3704	
Gibb Creek Machine Shop	GM	GCM General Stores	3705	
Gibb Creek Warehouse	GW	GCM General Stores	3705	Here two legacy ID map onto one new ID. This is a M:1
Farnham Bay Store	FS	Farnham Bay	5602	
Waring Bro's Fabricators	WB	Farnham Bay	5602	

Single Cross Reference Table: As with the Equipment Type example, we could review each Equipment Item and decide where it belongs in the new Equipment Location schema, thus creating an Equipment Item–Equipment Location cross-reference table prior to data load time. The load program would then read the cross-reference table for each item encountered and write the correct Location ID into the new Equipment table as it is created.

Default to M:1 with exceptions: When we look at the data in detail, we find that 70% of legacy Equipment Items have Site IDs that map 1:1 with new Equipment Location IDs. There are 25% of cases where the legacy Sites are being combined (ie are M:1) into a single Location ID and only 5% where a decision has to be made as to which new Location an old Site ID should be changed to (ie 1:M). In this case we may decide to run the load program with an Old Site–New Site cross-reference table and where Equipment Location records are found that could belong to more than one new Location we default them to a designated Location. A report is created that allows the users to correct the system post implementation. This illustrates the value of observing Golden Rule 3. A solution that is good enough but less than perfect is often acceptable. In this case provided there is enough ancillary data to get the right worker to the right machine for maintenance purposes we can settle for sub-optimal data in the medium term.

> **Hint**
>
> In this example because we know which Sites are being split into multiple Locations we would be more likely to extract those Equipment records that belong to Sites

> that are being recorded as many Locations and prepare them separately. However, in the real world, M:M are not always so easy to separate in advance of the load, especially where the navigation is complex.

This is the stage where a Data Quality Rules exercise should be carried out to decide the best way forward. As a Data Migration Analyst you can provide the data analysis of the percentages of records that fall into each category to inform the decision-making process. The Data Store Owner and Business Domain Expert need to be involved to tell you what is permissible and what is possible from an enterprise perspective. The Technical Data Experts and the Programme Experts will confirm what is needed technically and possibly the Audit and Regulatory Experts need to be consulted on what is required.

Hint

It is often tempting at this point to go for the 'obvious' technical option. This usually involves dumping a whole lot of work on the user population because, hey, the records failed validation didn't they? The users are either asked to sift, unaided, through a pile of rejected records or expected to prepare a population of records, again with little support. The difficulty of this data preparation is often compounded by the fact that the new system will have its own set of nomenclature and definitions. These may not have been briefed out. The results of a poorly motivated, poorly trained, poorly briefed, poorly supported workforce carrying out a data review and preparation under tight time pressure are often – poor!

Syncretistic option: Usually the one that prevails either wittingly or unwittingly. Syncretistic means 'made up of parts' and here I use it to cover the mixing of a bit of data preparation, a bit of error handling and record rejection at load time, with a bit of defaulting in valid values and a recovery exercise after the event.

Whatever option you choose, make it a conscious choice. And the earlier you are aware that a choice needs to be made, the better prepared you are to pick, not an option forced upon you by time pressures and circumstances, but an option both the technical and the enterprise sides are proud to live with. Read the remainder of this book – especially the model project section – and you will see how to best set up your project so that it meets that ideal.

Equipment Owner: This is an optional field in the Equipment table, reserved for those items of equipment that the enterprise does not own directly but uses, manages and maintains (like lease hire cars for example).

From our gap analysis we have identified a Legacy Data Store that will do the job.

Now we therefore have a tenable navigation. We need to:

- move the Lessor Spreadsheet data to a location that is searchable by our migration tool;

- we need to check for an entry on the Lessor Spreadsheet as each Equipment Item is read in;

- read a second cross-reference table because the Owner Code is different from the local code being used by the originator of the spreadsheet (but it is 1:1);

- apply the correct value to the Equipment Owner field.

We will probably also need a Data Transitional Rule to operate between the time we take a copy of the spreadsheet and the date the new system goes live to capture changes to the spreadsheet.

Input By: All new records on the Equipment table are to be tracked back to the person who created them for audit purposes. For the sake of completeness, and for Fallback we will know which of the multiple anticipated runs of our load program created a record. It has been agreed therefore that Input By will be a concatenation of 'DM' and the run date. This means that dummy employee records will need to be created for each run.

This is a simple example of concatenation. Often a new field needs to be made of two old fields (M:1) or one old field is split (also known as 'parsed') over more than one new field (1:M). There are also cases where two or more fields are parsed then concatenated over two or more new fields (M:M). Each field of course has its own validation and navigation rules which can be a compound of the examples above. Data mapping can become very complex – it is not often as easy as lifting one set of data from a Legacy Data Store and placing it into the new system.

Anecdote

The real-life experience on which this example is based included whole Equipment Items being split into more than one Equipment Item for maintenance purposes (1:M), and multiple Equipment Items being combined into single Equipment Items (M:1) on the basis of smallest maintainable unit. There were even situations, in some of the more complex engineering processes, where two existing Equipment Items

> became five new Equipment records (M:M) to better reflect maintenance rules. However, the principles remain the same – enlist your Data Stakeholder; express the problem in enterprise terms; seek out other Legacy Data Stores to help; complete a Data Quality Rules exercise; update the Data Mapping rules

Operator, Warranty Date, Warranty Description: These we are leaving blank. The Operator field is a transient data item (in other words its value changes regularly), in this case possibly more than once a day. It would not be possible to prefill it at system load time. The Warranty fields come with the new system and are new to the enterprise. Because the enterprise has never held this data before, there is no Legacy Data Store to get the information from. It has been decided that once the system is up and running an audit of purchase records will be made and the local managers responsible for Equipment maintenance will be responsible for updating it. This has, of course, been agreed with the Data Store Owner and Business Domain Expert. Had it been decided that the information was needed prior to the system going live, then a Transient Data Store would have had to be built to house the legacy Equipment Item ID and the Warranty Date and Warranty Description. A Data Transitional Rule would have been needed to keep the data store up to date.

Account Code: This is a straight 1:1 with the legacy Equipment Item Cost Centre Code. However, our Data Quality Rule work has shown that the data in it is only 97% correct. Some plant with a long working life still has cost centre codes that relate to a previous accounting package. Because the Equipment Item table was not linked to the accounting system, being out of step did not matter enough to the business for them to correct it. Our new system, however, needs accurate Account Codes because the new link to the maintenance system means that work has to be charged against the right Account. After running a Data Quality Rule workshop with the Data Store Owner and Business Domain Experts it was agreed that updating the legacy Equipment Item table was not tenable because of the awkwardness of the Legacy Data Store that held the Equipment Item table. The favoured alternative was to error out the records that fail to provide a valid Cost Centre Code at data load time and amend these in the soft copy. A piece of software has been written especially to allow the users to do this. The amended records will be resubmitted in a secondary run. Business Domain Experts are primed and will be standing by to carry out this task.

> **Hint**
>
> In reality it is extremely unlikely that we would proceed with a data load knowing as many as 3% of the key records would fail to load over something as easy to correct as a single coded value. What I am illustrating here is that because we have already evaluated the data quality via our Data Quality Rules there will be no surprises. Where the navigation transformation and validation rules are complex, rejecting records at data load time can be an expedient way of identifying those records that need enhancing. Where we do not want to be is in the position a lot of migration projects find themselves, where wholesale validation failures are not identified until the data migration is run for real.

Table 6.7 shows what the (partially) completed Data Mapping Table might look like:

> **Hint**
>
> It is normal, in fact almost universally applied, that a senior end user signs the mapping off at this point. On a major programme where possibly many hundreds of mapping tables with complex validation, navigation and transformation are being sanctioned this is not an insignificant bottleneck. Each complex operation must be explained and justified etc. If we have followed the steps above though, the Data Store Owner will have made the journey with us, making the sign-off that much easier. So although it may seem expedient to go for obvious solutions to mapping issues then place the finished article before the user population, experience shows that it is not. If you compound this by tying the sign-off to some late point on the delivery time line, you increase the risk of compromising end dates, quality and user–technologist relationships when your working assumptions are challenged.

This is not enough, however, to hand over to your programming team for them to write code and to your test team for them to develop their system tests from. It barely expresses sequencing rules or Windows of Opportunity. We need more. We do have the imperatives from the System Retirement Polices, plus the knowledge of our Technical and Programme Experts, but there are other aspects that need to be dealt with. These will be covered in the next chapter.

TABLE 6.7 *Whole Data Mapping table*

Target							Legacy Data Store		
Table Name	Field Name	Field Type	Field Length	Mandatory	Description	Validation	Transformation/Navigation	Source Name	Field Name
Equipment	Equipment ID	Integer		Y	Primary Key	Must be unique across the Equipment Table		System generated	
	Description	Character	200	N	Free Text	None		Equipment Item	Description
	Type	Integer		Y	Key of Equipment Type File	Must exist on the Equipment Type File	Link to user entered data in Equipment Cross Reference using original Equipment Item ID	Equipment Item/Equipment Cross Reference	See Transformation
	Status	Character	2		In Use; Obsolete: Scrapped; On Standby etc	Must exist on the Equipment Status File	Link to Equipment Status Cross Reference using Equipment Item Status ID to find the new Status	Equipment Item/Equipment Status Cross Reference	See Transformation
	Location ID	Integer		Y	Key Of Location File	Must exist on Location File with Status set to 'Operational', 'Mothballed' or 'Stand By'	Use Site on original Equipment Item to get a new value from Location Cross Reference File. Where this returns more than one value, use the first record and write a record to the Equipment Location Control File for later manual correction.	Equipment Item/Location Cross Reference	See Transformation
	Owner	Character	8	N	Key Of Owner File (some equipment assets are owned by third parties but maintained by us)	Must exist as Owner on Owner File with Status set to 'Current'	Use Item ID on original Equipment Item to check for value in Lessor table. If a match is found lookup the Owner ID in the Lessor/Owner ID Cross Reference File	Equipment Item/Owner Cross Reference	See Transformation
	Input By	Character	8	Y	Key of Emplyee File	Must exist as Employee on Employee File with Status set to 'Employed'	Will be a concatenation of 'DM' and the Migration Cycle	None	
	Operator	Character	8	N	Key of Emplyee File	Must exist as Employee on Employee File with Status set to 'Employed'	Leave blank		
	Warranty Date	Date		N	Date warranty expires (inclusive date)		Leave blank		
	Warranty Description	Character	200	N		Mandatory if Warranty Date Not Null	Leave blank		
	Account Code	Integer		Y	Key of the Asset Account File	Must exist on the Asset Account File with a status of Active		Equipment Item	Cost Centre Code

Chapter review

In this chapter you were introduced to:
- *comparing data structures;*
- *data gap analysis;*
- *Data Mapping (and ETL).*

To understand the choices we were introduced to:
- *data selection;*
- *data navigation;*
- *source to target ratios.*

7 Non-functional Requirements

In this chapter we will look at non-functional requirements. This will include:
- *data sizing;*
- *run times;*
- *sequencing;*
- *hardware and software considerations;*
- *Windows of Opportunity;*
- *Data Migration Implementation Forms;*
- *Fallback;*
- *The 'One Way Street' Problem.*

INTRODUCTION

'Non-functional requirements' is a term that is growing in popularity across the IT world. But as with a lot of terms, no two IT departments or consultancies can quite agree on what constitutes non-functional requirements. What follows is not an exhaustive list and even this list strays into areas that are not really the domain of data migration. Do not be surprised if an additional non-functional requirement is added to the list in your environment. However, there are some aspects peculiar to data migration that you will be expected to deliver to the system designers and programmers. Also taken with the preceding chapter they lead on to explain the dreaded 'One Way Street' Problem.

Hint

I prefer to steer away from the term 'non-functional requirements' on the assumption that all requirements perform some function or they would not be requirements, but I can see I'm losing the battle.

DATA SIZING

Data size

Data size is the amount of data to be loaded.

When designing the data migration event, the question of how big it is becomes significant. It is the biggest single determinant of the run times (see below).

Data size is normally expressed in bytes, kilobytes, gigabytes and terabytes as we go up the order of size. However, we can also measure data in terms of the number of records to be read and written. The number to be read is often far more than the number actually written, but reading takes time too. Complex data navigation can involve reading a score of records before a single record is written to the new system.

From our Legacy Data Store definition forms we will have captured the gross numbers of records in each data store. From our Data Mappings we will know the navigation involved and the consequent number of intermediary records we will be hitting. And from our System Retirement Policy and the new system definition we will know how many records we are expecting to load. From this information we will be able to calculate the size of the data load.

Hint

I say 'we'; of course I mean the technical experts. It is rare these days that a formal access path calculation is performed. We work on good guesses to assess the time it will take, but all the factors above are fed in to that guess.

It is not only the run times that need this input – any Transient Data Stores created at go live, the new system and the extract, transform and load process will all use space on our hardware. Temporary tables will be created, temporary indexes need space etc. We need to know both the size in bytes and the number of records to pass on to the programmers and database designers.

RUN TIMES

Run time

Run time is the length of time to execute a data migration extract, transform and load program.

When planning your data migration, how long it will take to run is key to defining your Windows of Opportunity even, possibly, your Data Migration Implementation Form (see page 103). The biggest single factor determining the run time is the data sizing. However, it is not the only determinant of how long the migration will take. The software used makes a big difference. Extract, transform and load tools are normally slower to execute than optimized bespoke code by quite a factor. Their advantage is that they are easier and quicker to write, often using 'point and click' interfaces that make for fewer programming bugs. But what you gain on the development side you lose on the run times.

Different computers run at different processor speeds and some operating systems are faster than others.

Some databases have very efficient load utilities, but often you are constrained by having to use a load utility (program) provided by the new system software supplier because it will perform all the appropriate validation.

Anecdote

I have quite successfully executed data migration using software that aped the activities of someone entering the data manually. This had the advantage of preventing us from having to learn all the complexities of an enormously involved database. But it was very slow. However, with relatively low data volumes the trade-off was worth it.

Whatever load software you choose (even manual data entry takes time – but we do not usually call that run time) the same software can be written well or badly. It can take maximum advantage of features in the software or it can be written very inefficiently indeed.

Anecdote

I was consulting on one project where by employing a skilled database administrator (DBA) for one day we reduced the run time of one piece of software from eight hours to 45 minutes. The moral is, find the appropriate Technical Data Experts for both the target and the Legacy Data Stores.

However, software run times are not the only consideration in fixing the time you need for your Window of Opportunity. Do not forget all the manual preparation that you are expecting to occur: the time that will elapse as you take your Check Points (see page 109) and often the time taken to physically courier data from its source to your processing centre.

SEQUENCING

Sequencing

Sequencing is the ordering of update processes into a tenable progression.

There is usually a sequence of updates that must take place in a known order. In our worked example we cannot create an Absence record before we have the matching Absence Reason and Calendar records to which it relates. This dictates the sequence in which the data must be loaded.

> **Hint**
>
> These data items from which everything else hangs are commonly called framework data and are also known as static data (because the data does not change much) and non-volatile data (for the same reason). The opposite is known as transactional data or volatile data or dynamic data. And, yes, there are another half dozen terms for each in existence. Once again, if in doubt, ask.

Churn rates will also affect your decision.

> **Churn**
>
> Churn is the relative frequency with which records of different types are added, amended or deleted from a data store.

You will get a first good estimate of the volatility (or churn) of each data item from looking at the Legacy Data Store definitions.

However, you must also consult with the new system Technical Data Experts. The new system will have its own way of processing and the new business systems it supports may alter churn. These factors may alter your data migration load sequence. If there are very low churn rates amongst some data items then you might consider loading them in advance of the main load. In our worked example the Location conceptual entity has a low churn. The enterprise does not add new premises very often and the subdivisions within the buildings are acknowledged to be stable. You will need to institute Data Transitional Rules to make sure that if there are changes these are reflected in the new system.

Another set of data items that can be loaded in advance of the big day are those that are peculiar to the new system. These are typically code items.

Commercial or other reasons can also influence sequencing. Not all business cycles run to the same timetable and some data items may be available to be moved before others.

There are also human resource and physical constraints that can affect sequencing. If the same set of Business Domain Experts is needed to perform more than one manual audit then the two audits will need to be moved apart. Even in today's world of email and easy communication we still find that we migrate data that is travelling from afar. This will be scheduled later in our plan if possible.

Finally, just as some data items can only be loaded according to a strict sequence, others can be loaded in parallel. We might add these in, just because we can, where processing is light.

All these considerations will alter the sequence we employ in our data migration design.

HARDWARE AND SOFTWARE CONSIDERATIONS

Few of us will ever have the luxury of deciding what hardware and software we will be working with. Most of us are stuck with what we are given. But each combination has its strengths and weaknesses. As you will, by now, be aware, once you have compiled your Legacy Data Store catalogue you (and your managers) may be amazed at the variety of data stores out there. We will have recorded the hardware and software types on our Legacy Data Stores definition forms, where we will also have identified the Technical Data Experts best equipped to help us. When it comes to getting the best out of the enterprise's data we will be in a strong position.

WINDOWS OF OPPORTUNITY

Most business processes go in cycles. We all know about the statutory reporting cycle, with the big hiatus at financial year-end when after a mad rush to process as many orders as possible the world stops whilst we wait for the year-end processes to run. But there are other cycles as well. Within those cycles exist the spaces of time when we can get access to the strategic Legacy Data Stores from which we will be getting large amounts of our data. It is quite often the existence of this window that determines the time frame within which we operate. We must have our data ready for the year- or quarter-end.

Anecdote

It is not just the business cycle that can determine the end date of the project. Long bank holiday weekends are another favourite time for migration exercises. I'm afraid that the quiet days between Christmas and New Year are often my busiest period, when most staff are off and there is plenty of spare capacity on machines. Like great chefs, data migration experts often work hardest when their clients are enjoying themselves.

Being tied to a Window of Opportunity is one of the many reasons why data migration projects are so often time based. We cannot afford to overrun when it may be 12 months before the ideal time comes around again. We must be ready on the night. It is an old maxim that there are four variables when it comes to software development – time, quality, experience and resources.

Time we can often do nothing about. The business case and the Window of Opportunity fix the time line.

We can maximize the depth of experience at our disposal by performing our Data Stakeholder analysis correctly. Also, the more migration exercises you perform, clearly the better you become at it. You have also improved your expertise by buying this book. Study it well.

Anecdote

Be wary of employing too many new technologies at the same time. There is only so much expertise to spread around. I was consulting at a large food processor who, on top of implementing a large migration that brought together many existing systems, also implemented a new integration tool at the same time. The idea was to use the Enterprise Application Integration tool to aid with the migration. Aside from it not being an appropriate tool for the job, the learning curve on top of the stress of coping with a significant implementation proved too much. We ended up loading the data using database scripts.

This of course does not cover the expertise you will need in the target system, but in my experience that is often not in short supply. From before the signature is dry on the contract the supplier, and the rest of the IT industry, will be offering technical experts. All that limits you is the size of your budget. Getting experts in your Legacy Data Stores is usually the bigger challenge. However, newly equipped with your Data Stakeholder analysis skills you will be way ahead of the field.

Of course it is one thing knowing when the Window of Opportunity is – when it starts and when it finishes – it is quite another to shoehorn all your data extraction, data preparation, data cleansing, bridging data gaps etc into the short space of time available. Never mind the run times associated with data loads. You need to have carefully calculated how long it will take to actually run the extracts and loads.

In the next section I talk about the various forms of data migration and how some are more dependent on tight timetabling. However, it is worth reiterating that by building a virtual team with your Data Store Owners and scrupulously observing the first Golden Rule of data migration, tight time scales can suddenly become loosened. Make it a business not a technical problem. Use it to discuss the form the data migration might take.

The quantity of resources, both technical and human, is often something you may have to fight for. It is quite normal for data migration to be the Cinderella of the programme (at least at first). Again, work with your key Data Stakeholders to reach acceptable solutions to your issues.

> **Hint**
>
> Of course resources can occasionally be an issue the other way round, when you are flooded with people, especially the wrong sort of people. When this happens, it is usually at the end of the programme, as technical staff start to become available. To protect yourself you need to have a robust resource plan and clearly identified Data Stakeholder roles. Chapter 3 will have helped you identify the correct roles, and Part Two will show you how to use the elements in this approach to create a coherent project plan correctly resourced.

So you may be able to do something about experience and resources. By leveraging your relationship with the Data Stakeholders and getting them to own both the problem and the solution you may get some flexibility over shut-down times. That leaves quality. Generally it is assumed that as the other variables shrink, so does quality. And that is a pretty fair assumption. However, we are adhering to Golden Rule 3. We expect that we will need to compromise on quality. We have built an influential team that is conscious of the necessity to prioritize one quality objective over another. Because of our Data Quality Rules exercises and our regard for Golden Rule 4 we will know where the data quality challenges lie. We will assist the enterprise in making mature data quality compromises that fit in with the other imperatives.

DATA MIGRATION IMPLEMENTATION FORMS

There are a number of types of data migration:

- **Big Bang Implementation:** This is the all or nothing approach where all the data is migrated 'on the night' and the Legacy Data Stores are all switched off.

- **Parallel Running Implementation:** The data is loaded onto the new system but the Legacy Data Stores continue to operate until the Data Store Owners are satisfied that the new system is a success.

- **Phased Delivery:** This can mean either loading only the data the business needs to go live, then adding history and other reporting data, or partitioning the whole project by some meaningful business grouping.

In addition to these, a pilot may also sometimes be run to work out timings and provide reassurance that the whole migration can be completed. This can precede any of the above migration forms.

Big Bang Implementation

Big Bang Implementation is in some ways the simplest and most obvious option. It is also the highest risk. If things go wrong then you are reliant on executing your Fallback strategy. Fallback strategies (see page 108) can be as complex and prone to error as the load process in the first place. Fallback strategies almost always involve designing and implementing more Data Transitional Rules so that transactions can be unravelled and reapplied. Big Bang Implementation is often, however, the cheapest. The enterprise is not paying for twice the physical machine space it requires, twice the licence fees and all the kindred add-on costs in terms of human resources etc.

Another advantage is that by not having to enter data into two different systems that may have quite distinct underlying data structures and reporting mechanisms you are not creating the problem of explaining apparent differences caused by processing and timing differences to perplexed key Data Stakeholders.

Parallel Running Implementation

Parallel Running Implementation is usually the most expensive but also the least risk form. If things go wrong then you can always revert back to your Legacy Data Stores that will have been maintained all along. It involves considerable expense in terms of dual provision of hardware and software and the personnel to run it. This is the option best suited to the risk-averse and for applications that really are mission- or safety-critical. To implement a parallel run, however, you may not need to brief out quite so many Data Transitional Rules. You will still need to cover transactions that span the go live period, but as you will be using Legacy Data Stores to cover your Fallback position, you will not need additional Data Transitional Rules to facilitate Fallback.

Phased Delivery

In this option the project will load only part of the legacy data set then add additional parts over time, until a full data set is loaded. This might be done for a number of reasons:

- The scale of the task means that there is not the management or other human resources to control the project on top of continuing to run the enterprise.

- There is such a degree of diversity in the Legacy Data Stores that bringing them all to the same level of data quality at the same time would be more complex than moving data in discrete chunks. This diversity could be geographical or logical. Many companies as they convert to enterprise retail planning type applications migrate sections of their enterprise at a time.

Anecdote

In the example on the previous page, each of the maintenance regions had been run as autonomous mini-enterprises. They had no Legacy Data Stores in common and faced quite different data quality issues.

- The Window of Opportunity is so small that time constraints force you to load only the minimum amount of data to get the enterprise up and running again and the enterprise is prepared to wait for the reporting and history items.

Then there are the not-so-plausible reasons:

- To save money – it probably will not save you money to continue to divert management and other human resources away from the day job for an extended period. Do the sums, but remember to include the opportunity cost of not being able to move the business forward as you wait for all the business to be rebuilt to the same model, and the cost of not using some of your best people elsewhere.

- To reduce risk – the longer any project goes on, the greater the risk. The commercial environment may change, technology may change, and project staff may get bored and move on. Also you are not going to be doing one data migration with all the risks that entails, you will be doing multiple migrations. OK, so you should be better at them by the time you get to the end, but there is still always the chance of hardware or software failure.

- The immovable end date approaches and some parts of the design, or heaven forbid the data migration, are not ready. If you follow the procedures in this book then you should never be in the latter position as the enterprise will have had to reconcile their objectives with you acting as honest broker. For whatever reason it has happened, although you should always obey Golden Rule 2, it behoves you to express as strongly as you can the risks that are involved with a Phased Delivery, especially an unplanned one. This is the worst reason for staggering migrations. It has all the risks of expediency that we are trying to avoid.

Phased Delivery is really best applied in environments of very large scale, where there are clearly distinct business segments that can be migrated separately. In those cases, far from making the task more complicated, you may find that a staggered approach allows you to simplify some of the logistical and planning issues.

> **Hint**
>
> Phased Delivery is most obviously appropriate in multinational projects. Crossing continents even in these days of rapid travel and instantaneous communications still presents all kinds of project challenges.

But such a form of migration is not without its own risks:

- The enterprise may move on, leaving some parts working to different processes or with different data structures.

- Executive attention may wander. We all know that high level sponsorship is the key to any project's success. You will have spent a long time cultivating your key Data Stakeholders but there is no guarantee that, over an extended period, you will not lose one or two and their successors may not have the same views on enterprise priorities.

- Each Key Business Data Area may need to have its own group of Data Stakeholders, and each group may have conflicting views on the enterprise's data quality priorities. This is less of a problem where the migration is phased over different conceptual entities (for example Accounts followed by Human Resources, followed by Work Planning). Where the split is geographical but the conceptual entities are the same and the migration is phased then there is a risk that inconsistent Data Quality Rules will be applied to the same conceptual entities from different geographical areas. This will undermine the data quality coherence of the delivered system.

> **Hint**
>
> The 'Not invented here' syndrome is probably one of the most basic and universal. Do not look at it as entirely negative. It is, after all, engagement of a type and the most vociferous protagonists will often become your greatest champions with the right encouragement. Get these people in the team as Business Domain Experts for their own migration. Let them have their say. There

> are still key decisions to be made regarding Legacy Data
> Store selection, Data Quality Rules etc. You will also
> find that, after the first or second iteration, your
> terminology of Data Stakeholders and Data Quality
> Rules will have gone feral. It may be easier in later
> iterations to get the right people on board, especially if
> the enterprise grapevine is telling tales of success,
> challenge, empowerment and fun.

You will have to pay close attention to your Data Transitional Rules. Indeed, if the process is protracted enough, these Transitional Rules will start to take on the air of permanence. There will be some parts of the enterprise in one state, some in another and some in transition. It may seem sensible to approach the data migration as a series of projects, but there has to be some coherence of those Data Transitional Rules that are needed to span the whole project life cycle.

Pilot implementation

I personally really like it when we are given the chance to pilot the implementation prior to the big event. We can check our timings, check our software (well it would have been tested first, but more testing is never a bad thing) and test our Data Transitional Rules. If we are smart enough, we can also test our Fallback arrangements (see the next page).

Approach a pilot as if it were the real thing.

Hint

It is tempting to go into a pilot as if it were a final testing phase. This is not a good idea. You will not increase your credibility within the enterprise by being responsible for a shambling exhibition of poor planning and poor execution. I know it is impossible to recreate the adrenaline-induced excitement of a real migration when possibly millions of pounds of capital cost is riding on a successful outcome, but you really do have to try.

Test out your briefing apparatus, your lines of communication to your key Data Stakeholders, take your Check Points, and run your Data Quality Rules, enact your System Retirement Policies. Involve your Data Stakeholders as much as you can. This can be an exciting and fun event. Don't forget to publicize your success.

Hint

If you have to revise any of the execution parameters because of over-long run times or for some other reason, make a positive thing of it and involve the enterprise Data Stakeholders in the discussion. They may not be able to contribute much technically but it shows respect for them and by witnessing the degree of intellectual effort that goes into the technical side of IT it will have the reciprocal effect of increasing their respect for you. (It may also encourage them to loosen the time constraints enough to allow your migration to proceed as planned.)

FALLBACK

Fallback

Fallback is the group of steps that will be taken to get the enterprise back into the position it was in prior to the data migration.

After having read this book you will of course be confident that nothing can go wrong with your migration, so why plan for something going wrong? Well the reasons are multiple.

- It provides reassurance to your sponsors and Data Store Owners that you have an alternative strategy.
- It may be a stipulation in a System Retirement Policy that normal functioning must be restored within a certain length of time. Having a fallback option allows you to guarantee that this obligation will be met.
- Software and hardware can go wrong or unforeseen circumstances can overtake the project on the night.

Anecdote

In one of my earliest go live experiences (not as a Data Migration Analyst) the power to the new computer room was cut by contractors working in the road outside, causing us to hold up implementation by two weeks while the power was reliably restored.

- Regulatory or legal requirements may mandate it.

Anecdote

This was especially the case when I was consulting to a company in an industry where a formal safety case had to be made, including Fallback, before the go-ahead could be given for a new system to go live.

So whatever reason you cite for getting the budget for creating your Fallback plan, make sure you do it.

Hint

Fallback, like car insurance, is one of those items that we pay for and hope never to use. Use the power of your Data Store Owners to create enough valid reasons to fund this necessary expense.

Of course when everything goes right on the night you will hope that the overwhelming feel-good factor, and the fact that your virtual team across the enterprise will be celebrating too, means that this redundant expense will be forgiven if not forgotten.

Anecdote

I have yet to have to execute a Fallback plan whilst I have been working on data migration projects but I recognize that one day I might.

What should a Fallback plan contain?

Fallback planning goes way beyond data migration. It includes human resources, physical implementation, housing, and legal and commercial issues. It also has business continuity and commercial implications. So, as with much else in this book, I will limit what I have to say to the areas affected by data migration.

Data Fallback, in essence, is the reverse of a data migration. We are taking data from the new system and rewriting it to the Legacy Data Stores from which it came. The scope of planning needed is affected by a number of variables:

- the Data Migration Implementation Form;
- the window agreed before the new system becomes accepted as being fully live and cannot be fallen back from;
- whether there has been a partial or full migration from Legacy Data Stores.

But all have certain features in common.

Check Points

> ### Check Points
>
> **Check Points (also sometimes known as 'go/no go points') are the decision points that it is agreed the new system is stable enough to go forward with or from which Fallback occurs.**

When you are designing your migration timetable, check through the System Retirement Policies for the key user acceptance tests that will show you when the migration has been a success. Group these by Key Business Data Area (because it is normal for data migrations to proceed in a sequence of Key Business Data Area loads). Gather together your major Data Store Owners and break the migration into sections meaningful both technologically and to the business. These then become your Check Points.

In our worked example, we may choose to load the Location Data first, followed by the Equipment then the Work Force then the Work Roster. The reason for making this choice is that it climbs the hierarchy of dependency. Location Data is fairly static and is not dependent on anything else. Equipment data cannot be loaded until the Location Data is present, but again it is fairly static and has no dependency on other conceptual entities. The Workforce follows because it also needs to have Location Data present. Finally Work Roster is loaded because it has the most complex relationships both with Equipment and Workforce.

After each stage of the load we will pause, validate that the data has loaded correctly by reference to the tests defined in our System Retirement Policies, then agree to move on. These will be our Check Points.

Check Points are best carried out by having a formal, minuted meeting between the relevant Data Stakeholders. From the enterprise side the Data Store Owners should be present and to aid them possibly the Business Domain Experts. From the programme side there should be the Technical Data Experts and the Programme Experts. On hand although not necessarily at the meeting there should be a clear contact line with the Corporate Data Architect. And of course you will be there to mediate and facilitate as the Data Migration Analyst.

The meeting should discuss only the checks in the System Retirement Policies (from a data migration perspective – the Programme and Technical Data Experts may bring issues in from their own viewpoints). This is not the time to introduce additional checks or allow vacillation. Provided the criteria in the System Retirement Policies are met, there should be no question about signing off that Check Point. If for some reason the System Retirement Policy requirements are not met then the meeting must decide if it is safe to proceed – always being mindful of Golden Rule 3.

If the decision is not to proceed then it is time to initiate the Fallback procedure. Otherwise you proceed from Check Point to Check Point.

Fallback forms

Just as there are different forms of migration, so there are different, although to an extent matching, forms of Fallback, influenced to a degree by the Data Migration Implementation Form.

- **Partial Fallback:** This is where we fall back as far as the previous Check Point, fix the problem, then attempt to reload. This is the commonest form of Fallback – often caused by some unforeseen software or hardware challenge, like the filling of index tables that will need to be cleared, resized then rerun.

- **Full Fallback:** This is where we completely abandon the migration exercise and restore to full working use the Legacy Data Stores. We would only do this under the most pressing of circumstances. It would mean that the whole migration was a failure.

- **Continue under caution:** It could be that the failure is minor or easily fixable therefore we can continue whilst acknowledging that additional work will have to be done. Getting the enterprise agreement to this is much easier if they are part of the virtual team. From the Data Quality Rules process they will have learned to prioritize so will be more amenable to considering a compromise. It is very important that at this point we are guided by Golden Rules 1 and 2, but there can be a conflict between our Data Stakeholders. This is where the programme sponsors will have to be brought into the debate.

- **Switch to Phased Delivery:** This is unlikely to be a planned Fallback position, although the distinction between proceed under caution and Phased Delivery is really a question of degree. It tends to suggest expediency – we are maybe trying to load data that we are not sure about. I strongly advise against this approach. It leads more often to disappointment and ruined IT–enterprise relations than success. Do your utmost to resist the 'chance your arm' approach to data migration.

Hint

You would be surprised how often this risky option is suggested, usually late in the timeline and usually to accommodate some late change. Get it discussed as widely as possible with the other Data Stakeholders that might be negatively affected. Given our strict adherence to Golden Rules 1 and 2 we will always bow to the wishes of the enterprise, but the way I see it, if the enterprise is prepared to live without the data loaded then wait until you can be certain it will load.

Fallback window

Fallback window

The length of time between starting up the new system and taking the final Check Point that allows for the full decommissioning of Legacy Data Stores according to the System Retirement Policies.

This is critical to the complexity of the Fallback process. Here we have a necessary contradiction. On the one hand there is the heartfelt need to keep a Fallback position in place until we are really confident that the migration has been successful and the new system is satisfactorily up and running. On the other, the more transactions that have been allowed to run through the new system, the more difficult it will be to reverse the new system data through the data migration transformation process.

There is a common misconception that if you can go one way through a set of algorithms then you can go always go the opposite way just as easily.

Anecdote

I have been told, on more than one occasion, by people who really should know better, that we could 'just run the code in reverse'.

Aside from the 'One Way Street' Problem illustrated on page 114, there is also the issue of reapplying transactions.

Transaction

A transaction in IT is the full set of database updates, applied in the correct sequence, that are needed to accomplish a business task.

In a computer system the physical updates are not allowed until the whole transaction is presented to the database. And they must be presented in the correct order. To use our worked example, if we are creating a new Worker record we must find a Manager, a Location and a Work Team to link it to. Then before the Worker can be created we must find at least one

Skill to link the Worker to. We create that link via a Qualification record. Unless the Worker Record and the Qualification record are created in the same transaction an error will be reported, but of course the correct sequence is Worker record first then Qualification record. It would make no sense to apply this in reverse.

If the new system has been running for a week, a great many transactions will have been carried out. Each one would need to be stripped out of the new system, turned around and reapplied to the Legacy Data Store. But here lies the problem, our Legacy Data Stores were not linked in the way the new system is. To reapply the transaction might require updates in multiple Legacy Data Stores. This problem is compounded by the mapping problems we discussed earlier. We would need a complete set of reverse mapping rules.

Given the cost of creating the mappings in the first place it is not likely that we would be given the opportunity to create a set going the other way. It is unlikely there would be a budget for it.

There are a number of possible solutions.

- **Data Transitional Rules:** We could create a set of Data Transitional Rules to cover the period from go live to final Check Point. These rules would put on one side, in a format that the Legacy Data Stores would recognize, copies of all the transactions we wished to possibly reapply.

  Once the final Check Point has been passed we can stop these Transient Data Rules.

> **Hint**
>
> You note I indicated only those 'we wished to possibly reapply'. Remember Golden Rule 3. Not every update carries the same value.

- **Parallel Running Implementation:** This provides us with the ultimate (if expensive) Fallback position. If the new system fails then we can go straight back to the Legacy Data Stores. These have been kept up to date because we have applied all the changes that occurred to the new system to them at the same time.

- **Retain original input:** This is really a variation on the Data Transitional Rules option except that where the original input is in the form of a paper record, we make sure we retain it. In our worked example the Daily Work Sheet was exactly that – a sheet of paper on which the workers recorded their day's activities. If we needed to Fallback we could take out boxes of saved worksheets and re-enter them into the Legacy Data Stores.

- **Reverse mapping rules:** This is the most complex option for the reasons indicated above. But it might be the most tenable depending on the complexity of the original rules and the absence of 'One Way Street' Problems.

Anecdote

The most difficult variation of this I have come across is where there was a Phased Delivery but a desire to leave a one week Fallback window. Not only was the new system being hit by thousands of transactions, the Legacy Data Stores were as well. The two systems were rapidly diverging so that it was not possible, even after one day, to reapply stored transactions and have the same effect on the legacy as on the new.

So which to choose? Each option has its risks and costs. Each needs to be evaluated in the circumstances of your migration. Leave plenty of time in your project plan to go through the options with your Data Store Owners. It may swing them behind a trial run if nothing else.

THE 'ONE WAY STREET' PROBLEM

The 'One Way Street' Problem

The 'One Way Street' Problem arises as a result of any algorithm that transforms data in such a way that the original values cannot be retrieved.

It might appear counter-intuitive that it is possible to so alter our data as we migrate it that it is impossible to go back the other way and recreate the original values. But it is. Anyone familiar with one-way encryption will be aware of how this can happen. But let us go through a worked example first.

Let us take the Equipment entity from our worked example as a demonstration. The new system allows us to create an Equipment hierarchy of any depth. However, to ensure consistency within our maintenance regime we are going to set a system constraint that will limit the hierarchy to three levels. There will be:

- an Asset level against which costs are gathered and which defines where the asset is located;
- a Maintainable Equipment level against which maintenance will be scheduled via the Job Sheet Lines;
- a Lowest Maintainable Part against which work will be carried out.

This is a bit like fixing the pump on the washing machine at home – you call someone out to your house to fix the washing machine and they

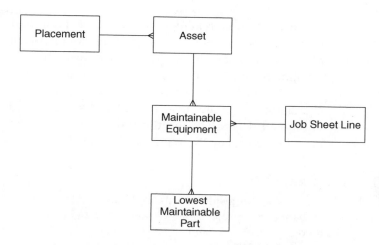

FIGURE 7.1 *New product structure*

replace the pump. The house would be the Asset, the washing machine the Maintainable Equipment and the pump the Lowest Maintainable Part.

We now have an entity model that looks like figure 7.1.

Now we know from the section on Data Mapping that the legacy Site ID had a M:M relationship to Placement. So we now have a set of have relations as in figure 7.2.

It is now no longer possible to get back from an Asset, a Maintainable Unit or a Lowest Maintainable Part to the Site where it originally was allocated, because the navigation from Placement to Site can give more than one answer.

Of course if we retain the Equipment Item to Equipment cross-reference table (if that had been the option we had chosen in our Data Mapping exercise) and kept a cross-reference between old Equipment Item IDs and new Equipment ID (which are system-generated), then the navigation becomes possible, at least for the Asset.

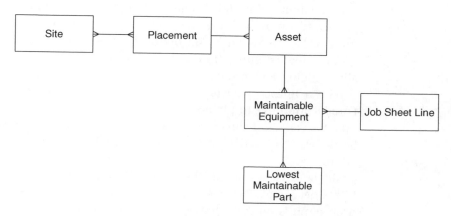

FIGURE 7.2 *The 'One Way Street'*

However, even retaining this level of audit trail does not solve the problem for reverse engineering at Maintainable Unit and Lowest Maintainable part level. They have lost their unique link back to Equipment/Site because it is now expressed as a relationship at Asset level.

In this case it would probably not be an issue unless there was a sudden change of design and it was decided that we should reorganize both the Equipment Hierarchy and the Placement and it was felt necessary to go back to the Legacy Data Store before moving forward again.

Anecdote

I make you aware of this problem because it caused me considerable pain at one project where it was requested that the accounts structure be reorganized. As you can see it can be tricky to explain even for a simple example. When there are a dozen or more steps in the transformation and the subsequent reverse navigation, it can be very difficult to see what has happened. Proving that something cannot be done is far harder than proving that it can.

This illustrates two points.

- It is possible to transform data by altering data relationships in such a way that it is impossible to go back even where the individual data items have not been changed.
- A full audit trail helps to alleviate the problem but does not necessarily solve it.

It is unlikely that you would encounter this under a Big Bang Implementation. Then either the new system has not gone live and you can start again, or if you are working from the new system, structural changes will take place by moving forward with the new system.

It is an issue where you are pursuing either a Phased Delivery or Parallel Running Implementation.

In a Parallel Running Implementation, where transactions have been processed by both the new systems and Legacy Data Stores, reloading from scratch may not be an option because it may not be clear against which reloaded entity transactions that take advantage of new functionality should be recorded.

With a Phased Delivery it is even more of a problem. At least with a Parallel Running Implementation if you are prepared to lose the novel updates you can Fallback and start again. With Phased Delivery there may be no way to Fallback and roll forward without a considerable manual effort.

All these issues should be factored into your Fallback and migration forms decisions. There is unfortunately no scientific answer as to how to proceed. It is unlikely that you will be able to maintain an audit trail that covers every update and only you have an idea of the likelihood of late changes. But in essence wherever the data migration exercise encounters a M:M condition there is always a risk that if you do not take sufficient precautions you will be stuck at the wrong end of a One Way Street!

Hint

Another reason for warning you about this is that you may be invited into a meeting with senior executives (and without notice) where you will be asked about the feasibility of Falling back for restructuring. It helps if you can lay down a marker for the future by saying that you will need to investigate further to safeguard them from the 'One Way Street' Problem. It may not make you popular at the time but this is where you can leverage the support of your virtual team.

Chapter review

In this chapter we looked at some of the non-functional requirements:
- *data sizing;*
- *churn;*
- *run times.*

We had a look at what influences these and how they help determine the size of the required Window of Opportunity.

From there we looked at Data Migration Implementation Forms and Fallback options including their Check Points

Finally we examined the One Way Street Problem.

Part Two
Specimen Project

8 Project Overview

This chapter gives an overview and introduction to the specimen data migration project that follows. It shows where the control points will be and explains how to use the tools in the previous section to build a bespoke migration project that will fulfil your unique requirements.

INTRODUCTION

What follows is a specimen data migration project strategy. It is intended to illustrate the use of the tools you have been shown. It is an Aunt Sally for illustration purposes. It is not meant to be my definitive word on what a data migration project should look like. It could be a useful basis for 'plain vanilla' data migration exercises where the standard paradigm of a new system replacing a plethora of existing systems is encountered. Any deviation from that – for instance where data has to be split because a part of a business is being spun off – would need a tweaking of the structure. It is my intention though to show you how to apply the tools outlined above in the most straightforward case, and trust that you can see where you need to make changes in the very specific circumstances that you find yourself.

On some issues I am very prescriptive.

- You must stick to the Golden Rules.
- You must identify your Data Store Owners and your Business Domain Experts.
- You must use Data Quality Rules to expose and correct data quality issues.

In other areas I think that there is more scope for variation:

- Choose your own type of data description.
- Choose one-pass or two-pass data preparation.
- Your project may be more iterative or more waterfall in style.

> **Hint**
>
> If you are not familiar with an iterative approach, I would recommend that you stick closer to the waterfall model – too many new approaches at one time are not to be recommended. Save the introduction of radical iteration for your next migration project.

- You may need to phase delivery and therefore run different stages in parallel.
- Data Transitional Rules may or may not be part of your deliverable. They may belong to the business change team on the project.

What I am giving you is a worked example that has, in my personal experience, taken real clients from data chaos to tidy new system. Use it to see the application of the tools above then bend it to the circumstances you find yourself in. The tools are flexible enough to allow you to put them into a framework more suited to your needs, but have faith in them and stick to the underlying principles of the data quest.

If you skimmed Part One Reasons and Methods then you might find yourself flicking back and forth to understand what is going on.

SPECIMEN PROJECT OVERVIEW

From the illustration on the following pages it can be seen that our specimen data migration project has four stages:

- Project Initiation;
- Stage 1 Data Preparation;
- Stage 2 Data Preparation;
- Stage 3 Build, Test and Go Live.

Each of these stages is briefly outlined below.

First, though, a brief digression to explain why I insist that data migration be set up as a separate project.

WHY A SEPARATE PROJECT?

Often it is the instinct of the programme manager to assume that data migration activities should be a part of the development effort. Multiple projects are just that much harder to manage, so why add complexity?

> **Hint**
>
> Nomenclature can be different in different working cultures. Often what would be a 'project' in one enterprise is classed as a 'work stream' in another. Whatever term is used to describe it in your environment, you need a distinct identity for the work you are carrying out in the data migration task for the reasons outlined below. For the sake of clarity the rest of this book will use the term 'project', but feel free to mentally substitute your own local phrase each time you encounter that word.

There are four main reasons why data migration should be managed as a distinct project:

- Data migration project products are different from the standard development ones.
- The data migration team mediates between the enterprise and the programme.
- Data Migration Analysts need specialized skills.
- The project structure of a data migration project is, of necessity, different from the structure of the main programme.

Migration products

As we have seen, there are a number of products that are unique to data migration:

- Data Quality Rules;
- System Retirement Policies;
- Data Transitional Rules;
- Data Stakeholder analysis.

The generation of these is best accomplished as distinct tasks, isolated from standard analysis and design activities, otherwise we risk over-burdening our client-facing opportunities and analysis resource. A meeting, conducted by a process analyst charged with understanding legacy operating procedures, becomes woolly and loses focus if it has to suddenly change track to consider Data Quality Rules. The nomenclature is different and the objective of the activity is different. One will produce swim lane diagrams, data flow diagrams, use cases or whatever process mapping deliverable the environment demands. A data migration workshop, on the other hand, will be producing Data Quality Rules, System Retirement Policies or Legacy Data Store definition forms.

Anecdote

Whilst working for one consultancy that specialized in the transport sector, I allowed myself to be persuaded that I could use the process analysis workshops to create Legacy Data Store forms and start on the Data Quality Rules process. It didn't work. The participants were tired after a long session mapping out their current processes and confused as to why we appeared to be starting again with similar questions just as it looked like they could head off home early. The idea was dropped and me along with it. The system went live, but the client was disappointed with the number of 'data issues' that bedevilled the early days of system use.

Mediation role

As part of the Data Stakeholder analysis we will find both business-side and programme-side experts. We will then mediate between them to produce the best quality data that both sides can accept, that matches business need, technology need, and time and money constraints.

We make our lives that much harder if we are not clearly seen as an honest broker between the two. And we make our lives impossible if we try to embody two roles – representing the technical side as well as mediating two legitimate but occasionally conflicting sets of requirements.

Anecdote

It is this confusion of roles that leads to many a data migration disaster. The risk of allowing the technological to overtake the enterprise – violating Golden Rules 1 and 2 – is almost impossible to avoid. We need the distance of being disinterested onlookers to allow us to help each side work through their possibly contradictory needs.

Distinct skills

To be a successful Data Migration Analyst requires a distinct mix of skills. On the one hand you need to be able to perform data analysis and data model composition. You should be capable of comparing data models of variant structure and spotting gaps and overlaps. On the other hand you need to be able to develop, almost on the fly, new, albeit temporary, business processes to fulfil your Data Quality Rules or Data Transitional Rules requirements. It is useful if you have a basic understanding of at least query level access to the technology with which you will be dealing. You will be good at interviewing and running workshops.

This is quite a mix. On most modern projects specialization has robbed us of the opportunity of practising the whole range of skills we might have trained in.

Anecdote

This is one of the reasons I was attracted to data migration as a career. I get to perform formal analysis and design, both process and data. I get to build small, lightweight, departmental systems from scratch (OK, so they get thrown away shortly afterwards, but I have the pleasure of building them). I get to meet and work closely with the real workers in the enterprise and build teams across departmental boundaries. Data migration is fun!

It also really aids a migration project, given that building the virtual team you will need for success is as important as any technical skill, if the same resource sticks with the same Key Business Data Area throughout. Of course resource churn is a fact of life on large, long-running projects, but it is not something to be encouraged. Placing data migration in the middle of other workstreams makes it everyone's and no one's responsibility. Each Key Business Data Area needs a champion to ensure that data of the appropriate quality and format reaches the bigger programme at the right time.

Hint

This is not to say that there are no benefits in using the talents of some of the technologists involved. Where a Corporate Data Architecture function exists, for example, with data models of Key Business Data Areas, then that is one less activity that the data migration team have to carry out. Use these resources if they are available but always under the control of the data migration project, not as diffuse projects in their own right.

What if I can't persuade the programme manager?

OK, so you've used all your powers of persuasion but your boss just will not buy running this as a separate project. Well, the easy answer is to skip straight to Chapter 13, hunker down and prepare for the worst!

However, short of walking out, most of us have to do something, if only to safeguard our mortgages and pensions.

Assuming that you have been given responsibility for data migration activity and are not shouting from the sidelines, you have to see how your data migration activities can be fitted in around normal analysis and design activity. But remember; this is the least worst case – the best and safest course of action is to follow the steps outlined in this book.

> **Hint**
>
> I am a big believer in the necessary underlying logic of reality – in other words, the same problems produce similar solutions eventually. Data Quality Rules, the search for Data Stakeholders, System Retirement Policies, gap analysis etc will emerge, albeit with different names, less rigorously defined and less well structured and probably too late.

A well-run project will have a change control process. Get your Legacy Data Store List placed under change control.

Most enterprises are aware of the data quality challenges in their Legacy Data Stores. In most development methods there is an investigation into the state of the current physical business processes and how they interact with the underlying data stores. Get yourself invited to those interviews/ facilitated workshops, but go with a data migration perspective. You are looking for the equivalent of first-pass Data Quality Rules.

Second-pass Data Quality Rules (even if they are not called such within your programme) are much more acceptable. Everyone accepts that there has to be some transformation of data as it moves from the Legacy Data Stores to the new system, and all IT practitioners are aware of the need for rigorous data validation routines. The challenge here, and one that this whole approach is designed to avoid, is that there is often no forethought as to what to do with the data that fails validation, other than to throw it back at the enterprise. Here you must work hard at ensuring that there is support for the enterprise or at least some business readiness activity.

Getting Data Store Owners assigned will be more difficult without the active support of the programme management. You will have to use your networking and influencing skills. Business Domain Experts tend to be a little easier to find. Most projects these days at least pay lip service to being customer-focused.

> **Hint**
>
> Here you may find that you are pushing at an open door. In the more old-fashioned IT-led programmes there is often a bunch of disgruntled Business Domain Experts who feel they are not being adequately listened to. Getting the best out of them whilst still keeping good relations with the larger programme will test your diplomatic skills to the maximum, however. You must not let your area become the hinterland for the disaffected programme assassin.

Creating System Retirement Polices without the active engagement of Data Store Owners is very difficult. The large enterprise systems will be covered by activities within the programme. Smaller departmental systems will be patchily covered, probably more by aspiration then a structured approach. Individual desktop applications will be ignored (probably). If they are covered at all it will be via a blanket sweep of all desktops by the foot soldiers of the IT department. This rarely permanently removes all local Legacy Data Stores. I am not sure that there is a recommendation to help here. It may be just one of those sub-optimal outcomes you have to accept when working from within the larger programme as opposed to managing your own project/work stream.

So still want to go ahead?

You may have little choice. What you have to do is try to work into your way of doing things as many of the aspects of this approach as you can. Renaming things can make a big difference and remember – it is the Golden Rules that are the most significant. Sticking with them in spirit will increase your chances of success. And good luck to you.

BACK TO THE EXAMPLE PROJECT

Project initiation

All successful projects start off with an organized project initiation phase and a data migration project is no different. There are organizational activities that must be attended to and there are political activities that if tackled at the outset will greatly increase your chances of success. This Stage will get you off on the right track. Do not try to skimp it.

Stage 1 Data Preparation: why two stages of data preparation?

There are two stages of data preparation because we must first analyse and fix the problems in the Legacy Data Stores and Key Business Data Areas before we can proceed to matching the data in the Key Business Data Areas to the structures in the new system design. It has always been my experience that there will be known and unknown problems with the Legacy Data Stores. Some data stores will have been built for specific local purposes and will not match the Key Business Data Area model. They will have no keys that match other data stores, they may not even have similar entities. We need to know all of this before we try to match the legacy data with the new system data. We will also need to fix some of these problems before we can begin to proceed to the second phase of data preparation.

Anecdote

I cannot tell you how often this is overlooked. Just about every data migration that runs into difficulty will have gone straight from the new design to the Legacy Data Stores and, based on a Key Business Data Area model view of the data in the Legacy Data Stores, made all sorts of assumptions. These assumptions may not have been tested until the first load of production data is applied to the test area. Then, when the budget has been spent and time is short, all the local idiosyncrasies of the Legacy Data Stores appear. (Sometimes these things do not show up until the night of the live data load, then, wow, do you have fun.) What follows shortly after is a descent into the familiar cycle of mutual recrimination, career damage, sleepless nights...

Also the first phase of data preparation can commence in parallel with ongoing new system design. This means all the virtual team building, finding of stakeholders and identification of Legacy Data Stores, creation of initial Data Quality Rules etc can be started as early as possible. These are not tasks that are dependent on the new system design being completed.

However you should be aware of the general direction of the new system design and allow this to inform your choice of focus for activities in this stage. If the programme's chief object is the integration of two merging companies' sales planning systems, then Legacy Data Stores concerned with stores replacement may be of interest, Legacy Data Stores concerned with audit compliance will probably not be. Always draw up a Legacy Data Store form and store it away in the programme library when a new store is encountered, but if a legacy data store has no matching conceptual entities within the Key Business Data Area(s) that is being migrated it can, probably, be excluded. Always remember Golden Rule 2 though, and check with the business.

It is within Stage 1 Data Preparation that the first-cut System Retirement Policies are produced. Although at this stage we may not know what the new system design will look like, System Retirement Policies focus the minds of the Key Stakeholders on the reality of the imminent demise of their systems. Getting a base line statement of what the key Data Stakeholders need before the Legacy Data Stores can be removed is vital to the planning of subsequent tasks. Do it thoroughly and do it early!

Hint

Use the phrase 'data preparation' as opposed to 'data cleansing'. After all, this may be someone's cherished data store, the result of a working lifetime. 'Data

cleansing' suggests that you are finding fault with it
before you start. Also it reminds everyone that this is a
data migration project and their data stores will be
migrated to the new environment.

Stage 2 Data Preparation

This is closer to the traditional starting point for data migration projects.
We will be better armed than most however because when we start to map
Legacy Data Stores onto new system design requirements, we will have
greater knowledge of the strengths and weaknesses of the Key Business
Data Areas and Legacy Data Stores.

We will:

- know where to get the best quality data;
- have the Data Store Owners identified and on side;
- have the Business Domain Experts identified and lined up to help us;
- have already polished the Legacy Data Stores so that they are, if not
  totally consistent with the Key Business Data Area rules at least
  inconsistent to a known degree.

Our intermediary deliverables will be more Data Quality Rules, completed
and signed off System Retirement Policies and a set of new system
business area Conceptual Entity Models (or whatever you are using in your
local environment to fulfil this modelling requirement). We will also,
possibly, be designing and building Transient Data Stores for the
transformation of Legacy Data Store data that cannot be prepared
adequately in situ.

We will also create the extract, transform and load definitions we will be
using as the basis of our migration design specifications. These may
include designs for Transient Data Stores, but only for those that are going
to be used for automated, 'on the day' transformations.

Stage 3 Build, Test and Go Live

This is where the nuts and bolts of the build and test activity for the
migration takes place. It will use as inputs extract, transform and load
definitions, the signed off System Retirement Policies that may specify
Legacy Data Repositories for legacy data that cannot be migrated, Data
Quality Rules documents and the new system design documentation.

This is the stage where we will build and test the load scripts and any
Legacy Data Repositories. We will contribute the data migration aspects to
the go live plan. We can expect that we will be creating Data Transitional
Rules as well.

Hint

Anticipate the need to create Data Transitional Rules by building time for them into your planning. It is almost inevitable that there will be a hangover of transactions started in Legacy Data Stores that must be completed in the new system.

Finally we will conduct a post-implementation debrief, accept the plaudits of our peers, the undying love of our business colleagues and the heartfelt thanks of our bosses. We can then roll up our sleeves and, as fully bloodied experts in the black art of data migration, expect that our next job down the pike will be another data migration exercise.

USE OF ITERATION

Within the data preparation stages it is expected that there will be a degree of iteration. There are a number of reasons for this. First of all the process of data preparation is naturally iterative. The first set of Data Quality Rules produced will normally be to investigate data quality issues or to quantify data quality based on the metrics stipulated within the Data Quality Rules. These will lead naturally on to a second set of Data Quality Rules that will endeavour to fix problems unearthed in the first.

Secondly in the real world where most of us work, we are not afforded the luxury of working in a vacuum unconstrained by what is going on in the rest of the programme. Data migration should be seen as a large and complicated process and planned as such at the outset of the programme. To get through all the work that is necessary and finish in line with new system delivery, we need to work in parallel with ongoing design and build work streams. Of necessity this will result in late design changes filtering through to the data migration project. We must anticipate this. As you can see we leave our dependency on new system design as late as possible, but – well you may work in a different world from me – I've never known late design changes not to occur! Worst still we may be the architects of our own problems by uncovering data issues that have been overlooked by the new system designers and that themselves cause design changes!

Finally, as I indicated in Part One Reasons and Methods, we must expect to uncover hidden data stores that are unknown to the programme (or indeed to the rest of the company sometimes). These will impact on the work we have done and require a new iteration.

PROJECT CONTROL POINTS AND PLANNING

The data migration project is segmented into stages because this allows for a formal replanning step between each stage.

To assist the project or business managers I have added paragraphs at the end of each stage description that illustrate where the management control points are. Again, if you rework the project structure, as you probably will, you will need to rethink these control points but you will find, if you use the same tools, that the same basic items are at the bottom of your product hierarchy even if the structure is different. They have been designed with project control in mind.

Within each stage there are a number of deliverables that can be planned. Care has been taken to define the products in such a way that tracking of activities is always possible.

Chapter review

In this chapter we had an overview of the specimen data migration strategy outlined in the chapters that follow. You are reminded that this is an illustration only and that you must develop a fresh strategy for each unique migration you face.

The use of iteration was introduced.

9 Stage 0 Project Initiation

This chapter describes the project initiation phase of an illustrative data migration project.

It shows that whatever shape your data migration project takes, a formal initiation with a migration strategy is mandatory. Within that strategy some items can be swapped with adequate local substitutes, others are obligatory.

INTRODUCTION

As we have seen in Chapter 8, a data migration exercise is best undertaken as a separate project within the wider new system implementation programme. As a stand-alone project it should be initiated as any stand-alone project within a larger programme would be. A data migration project is a significant piece of work and a formal start to any project makes a big positive difference to successful long-term outcomes.

STANDARD PROJECT INITIATION DELIVERABLES

I am not here to tell you things you already know but in case you feel that, as a project professional, you are sufficiently well versed in project initiation phases then I still recommend you read on. This is a project with some unique attributes, usually commenced after the main body of the programme has been running for some time. The complexity and effort required is generally underestimated. You have to make these risks and costs clear to the programme management.

Although most of the steps should be common to any project, they often have a special spin on them that requires a slightly different approach.

Although you can mix and match to an extent local deliverables with these data migration products, some items within this method are obligatory. And the first mandatory product is a data migration strategy document laying out how you will proceed.

CREATE YOUR OWN DATA MIGRATION STRATEGY

Well done – you've made a good first step by buying this book! Show it to your peers and bosses and get them to buy copies too. It may, on its own, convince them of the scale of the task you have been given. But enough of the sales pitch. If you do everything in this book, and follow not just the letter but also the spirit of the Golden Rules, you will have a successful data migration and no worries. However (and, yes, there has to be a caveat) I do not know anything about the environment in which you find yourself. It could be that some of the items outlined here have already been delivered elsewhere in your programme. For instance, historical data retention of data in Legacy Data Stores may have been covered by the analysis and design for the new system or by a separate work stream so there will be no need to replicate it in a new set of technical specifications. In that case make sure there is a reference to the programme documentation in each System Retirement Policy where it is appropriate.

Sometimes you find that the data migration project is very narrowly defined and that the system go live timetable is being managed elsewhere on the programme. In that case, check that the format of the System Retirement Policies will be acceptable to the team working in this area.

System Retirement Policies are essential to this approach, not just to provide the analysis on which the Physical Migration Design will be based, but also to draw the Key Data Stakeholders into ownership of the process of data migration. System Retirement Policies, or some substitute, must be started in Stage 1. Your data migration strategy must make clear how this is to be done, and who on the project is responsible for seeing that they are delivered. System Retirement Policies are also the place where user acceptance testing is first defined (for the data migration aspect). You need to liaise with the test team on your project so that the form and timing of your test requirements best fits with their needs.

Again, in many well-run projects there is a 'business readiness' work stream that will brief out changes to business procedures. If your programme has such a team, then fantastic – use them. Work out with them how to present your Data Transitional Rules to them so that they can brief them out to the business. Find out who they have identified as key contacts in the business. These people are often going to be your Business Domain Experts. But most of all, work out where there are areas of overlap. If they are available to do some of the interfacing with the enterprise then, fine, you do not have to, just make sure that your activities and theirs are complementary.

There may also be substitutions you need to make to various deliverables, for local policy reasons. I have discussed above the role of logical data models as my preference when defining and comparing Legacy Data Stores but suggested that they could be replaced if it is expedient. There are other features that you may find run foul of local standards, or additional documents you need to create for local audit reasons.

Also if your Data Stakeholders include a Corporate Data Architect then they may suggest and possibly mandate the use of certain methods and the production of certain deliverables. Resolve with them how your approach is going to fit into their architectural vision.

Sometimes it is useful to alter the nomenclature. For instance you will often find that there is a better, more readily acceptable local synonym for the rather inelegantly named Key Business Data Area. If there is, then use it but be sure it performs the same function.

Finally, when I embark on a significant data migration project there are some things I expect to find already established on the main programme – but I am often disappointed. I like to find change management but this is not always up and running before data migration commences. This is especially true where the project is almost purely migration-driven – like for instance when this migration is part of a company-wide standardization programme.

For all these reasons and also because if you follow this method you will be proceeding in a manner perhaps different from that expected, it is essential that you spell out up front what your version of this method is going to look like in your environment.

By all means use this document as a basis for you data migration strategy document or Project Initiation Document (PID) or whatever your local project method calls it, but tailor it to the needs of your programme and get the programme board to endorse it with their signatures. You need them to commit to supplying the data migration project with the support it will require to succeed.

Just as importantly, you need them to accept and understand the implications of the Golden Rules. This is especially true of Golden Rule 3: 'No organization needs, wants or will pay for perfect quality data'. Your project activities and project plan will be based on adhering to this. It allows you, in conjunction with Golden Rules 1 and 2, to work with the Data Stakeholders to prioritize your activities.

Identify the deliverables you will be receiving from the programme that will allow your data migration project to function. Match what the programme is expecting to deliver with what I have outlined in this book. Inform the programme what you expect to be delivering to them. Look for overlaps and gaps and alter you strategy accordingly. Do not be afraid to ask for additional resources, or additional deliverables from the programme so that you can complete your activities. Because you now have a structure to work to, if these resources are not forthcoming, then you have something to assess the risks and impacts against.

How far you share this data migration strategy with the other Data Stakeholders is more complicated. At this point you will not have identified all your Data Store Owners. This is really a project sponsor and programme management level document. These are the people that you have to convince that you have a way forward that will work, with some information on costs and timeframes. The Data Store Owners will be involved in due course via the Data Quality Rules and System Retirement Policy activities.

What must be included are the terms and definitions for the products discussed in this book that are non-standard within your environment. It is no use telling the programme board that you will be creating Data Quality Rules in Stage 2 but not telling them what they are! I only ask that you credit this book and this author when you use the terms described in this book.

FIRST-CUT PROJECT PLAN

A plan should be developed that shows the interdependencies of the deliverables within this work stream. Have a look at the control points in the following chapters and see how they match with your use of the tools in your strategy.

A plan should be developed that links the stages outlined in your data migration strategy to the deliverables coming out of the rest of the programme. This will protect you if (when?) there is slippage elsewhere in the programme.

Your plan will be very high level at the moment. You do not know the number or complexity of Data Quality Rules documents you will be creating for instance. It should be an indicative plan for Stage 1 Data Preparation based on the project brief you have been given plus time boxes for Stages 2 and 3 that will be filled later.

SET UP AN APPROPRIATE PROJECT SUPPORT OFFICE FUNCTION

This aspect of data migration projects is so often overlooked until things start to go wrong. Once again this is not an area that a book on data migration should try to cover exhaustively. There are plenty of books that cover project management. All I intend to address here are those aspects where a data migration project differs from the norm.

Environments differ but for me the most significant aspects to get a handle on are the configuration management and planning functions.

Configuration management

Configuration management is the process of holding a definition of the current state of the deliverables and being able to go forward to newer versions or revert to older ones. In a normal IT setting this is usually restricted to code and the version of the database to which that code relates. In a data migration project there will be code involved but there will also be, just as importantly, non-code items. I usually think of configuration management in terms of the configurable items I wish to place under control. In data migration projects the following non-code items should be controlled:

- the migration strategy;

- Legacy Data Store definition forms;
- the Legacy Data Store List;
- Data Quality Rules documents (once the facilitated meeting is over);
- System Retirement Policies;
- data models;
- Data Transitional Rules (where these are held separately from System Retirement Policies);
- extract, transform and load definitions;
- physical design specifications.

If your strategy replaces one of these forms with a local deliverable (for instance where the Legacy Data Store definition forms are held within a data migration tool), you must consider how you manage versioning of these items.

You must also know how changes to one item (for instance the new system data model) will be cascaded onto the other items (for instance System Retirement Policies) in a controlled manner.

I cannot attempt to specify how this will work in your environment. Some sites have sophisticated document management systems; some projects make do with a controlled library on a file server. As long as it fulfils the requirement of having a known repository that defines the current state, then it is good enough. But make sure it is spelt out in your strategy document.

Project planning

It is the responsibility of the project to feed back, both to the programme and to the key Data Stakeholders, where we are with our activities.

The project plans themselves can be in any format that you find appropriate. As I indicated above, I quite often use some form of graphical representation, not necessarily a Gantt chart. Keeping the Data Quality Rules autonomous and distinct helps reduce cross-dependencies and so keeps the planning simpler.

Most projects I have worked on are time-bound not activity-bound, by which I mean that the end date is given and can only be shifted at considerable pain and expense. Indeed the business case for the programme generally hinges on timely delivery.

Anecdote

When I say most, I really mean every single project I have been on. Not that all of them met their time objectives of course, but overruns are rarely excused by the task being more difficult than outlined in the business case.

We never really have the luxury of being able to take as much time as we might like to complete the activities outlined in the methodologies that are taught in college. The approach in this book takes account of this real-life fact by sharing the onus of compromise decisions amongst the Data Stakeholders.

For these reasons I prefer to create a time boxed plan, containing time frames for each of the other three phases outlined in this section. Where the project is a plain vanilla system replacement data migration, I line up the end of Stage 1 with the end of the analysis phase of the main development activity. Stage 2 therefore starts with the introduction of the new system data model. Stage 2 persists until the end of the new system development and Stage 3 is a relatively short period that parallels the main development testing and training phase. Because each stage ends with a re-planning step, you will have the opportunity to re-plan as you go along.

I usually advise that plans that are going to be presented to programme boards be as high level as possible. If detail is asked for then it can be readily given, because all metrics bubble up from the lower level items and obeying Golden Rule 4 all the lowest level items are objectively measurable, but presenting a plan of a couple of hundred rows is rarely informative.

Tracking itself should be at the lowest level. Reporting to concerned groups of Data Stakeholders can be at an intermediary level so that it is informative but not overwhelming. Between these objectives I build my project planning and reporting strategy. So, for instance, I may report to the programme board at Key Business Data Area level, to the business owners at Data Quality Rules level, but gather my information at individual Data Quality Rule task level.

At the end of each stage of this illustrative data migration strategy I show the deliverables that are the principal agents of control. The structure you use may be different from this one but as you will be using the same building blocks you should be able to use the same control elements within your project.

What is important is that we can report and everyone understands and agrees with the level of reporting they are going to receive.

I have been using project planning tools for years and find them useful, but do not mistake a fine project planning tool with a fine project plan. Better a bunch of spreadsheets accurately measuring deliverables that stick to the Golden Rules than a glitzy presentation of impressionistic values that measure nothing.

INITIAL LISTS OF DATA STORE OWNERS, LEGACY DATA STORES AND KEY BUSINESS DATA AREAS

It may seem inappropriate in a project initiation phase to be already getting on with the deliverables of the project, but in reality some of the initiating activities will, of necessity, have created or revealed a first-cut set of Legacy Data Stores, Data Store Owners and Key Business Data Areas. It would be churlish not to capture them to pass on to the next stage.

Your project brief should have included a statement of the Key Business Data Areas, or at least the business systems covered by the migration. Whether it does or it does not, one has to be included in your data migration strategy. This is your project scope and illustrates that you and the project sponsors share an understanding of what your area of operation is going to be. It is important that you express the Key Business Data Areas in business not computer system terms. From the outset you must present yourself as business- not technology-focussed. Of course in many organizations the two are so intrinsically linked that to create a distinction would be difficult. I leave it to you to decide how far you go down that route, but where there is a choice, use the business terminology.

Whether you merely name them or produce a first-cut data model is up to you. Stage 1 initiation is enhanced if you have models to brief out to those who will be joining at that stage, albeit that you caution them that the models are tentative. On the other hand it is definitely on the 'nice to have' end of priorities. Do not compromise prompt delivery of the data migration strategy waiting to get them developed.

> ### Hint
>
> **Items like first-cut data models for Key Business Data Areas produced at this point are likely to change (unless they originate from a reliable source like the Corporate Data Architecture team). I put them into appendixes in the original document. I then make plain that the appendixes are illustrative only and do not form part of the configurable item. That way as knowledge about them grows and they are enhanced the original document is not compromised and does not have to be reissued.**

When I arrive on a new data migration project there is often an expectation that I should just get on with it. There is often no expectation that I will be producing a strategy document. To buy time and to publicize the project I always declare an amnesty on the revelation of all those hidden data stores that are secretly running the business. Once the amnesty is over, any additional Legacy Data Stores have to go through our newly devised change control. This means that in the first weeks of the project, before the strategy is even agreed, we are already testing out our lines of communication and beginning to establish our virtual team. We are also publicizing the existence of our project. This amnesty will spill over into Stage 1 and is really a Stage 1 task brought forward for tactical reasons.

From the outset each Legacy Data Store that is identified to you either via the project initiation document or from your amnesty must be included on the Legacy Data Store List and have a Legacy Data Store definition form initiated for it.

Because Legacy Data Stores will emerge from the very beginning of the project, Data Store Owners will start to emerge and also, possibly, other Data Stakeholders. Log these on your Data Stakeholders list but treat them with caution, they all need to be investigated before you can confirm them in their role.

Test strategy

I would always recommend that at the earliest stage you start thinking about how your testing is going to be performed and what degree of the various types of testing you are anticipating. Are you considering Parallel Running? Will you be expected to perform your loading into live systems and so need to test the robustness of new software tools? Which combination of user, system and performance testing is expected in your environment? Do you have a discrete testing team and what are their expectations of inputs and test phases?

All these items should be considered now, even if there may be no conclusions until we have encountered the technology we will be using. At least we can create a place in the plan where decisions postponed now can be made. The inputs for the data migration tests will be the Data Quality Rules, the System Retirement Policies and the extract, transform and load documents.

> **Hint**
> There is considerable data quality testing built into this approach via the Stage 1 and Stage 2 Data Quality Rules activities. A reference to their role in this regard in the testing section of the data migration strategy document helps gain the programme board's trust.

STAGE 0 CLOSEDOWN

The most important single item to have completed at this point is the data migration strategy. It needs to spell out how you, in the commercial context you find yourself, are going to get the right data from the right sources to the right quality to the right place at the right time. It will include an indicative plan with replanning steps in it preceding each of the subsequent stages.

It will spell out what support you are expecting from the wider programme and what project office functions you are going to be calling on. It will also explain how your project is going to interface back into the wider programme and the format of inter-stream deliverables. The scope of a data migration project – both what it will include and what it will exclude – will be specified.

In addition you may have started some of the Stage 1 tasks early, so you may have a Conceptual Entity Model in embryo, some early Legacy Data Store definition forms, and the beginnings of your Data Stakeholder catalogue. These will be passed on to the next stage.

STAGE 0 PROJECT CONTROL POINTS

Only you will know how many days to allow for completing and getting signed off a data migration strategy document in your environment, but that will be your first control point.

Once you have agreed the format of your deliverables with the programme board, and the timing and format of the deliverables from the programme to the data migration project, you will have the framework of the plan within which you will work. Creating the plan and establishing the Project Support Office are the two remaining deliverables in Stage 0.

Chapter review

This chapter discussed the necessity of creating a data migration strategy to initiate the data migration project.

Essential items of a strategy are:
- *the scope of the project (Key Business Data Areas);*
- *the initial Data Stakeholders list;*
- *the structure of the project;*
- *which elements from this approach you will be using;*
- *which elements from this approach you will be substituting;*
- *the establishment of the project support office functions;*
- *the establishment of resource requirements;*
- *the creation of a plan for the next stages and inter-stream dependencies.*

Optional items are:
- *Key Business Data Area models;*
- *Legacy Data Store amnesty and definitions.*

10 Stage 1 Data Preparation

In this chapter you will be creating:
- *Legacy Data Store definitions;*
- *Key Business Data Area definitions;*
- *System Retirement Policies;*
- *Data Quality Rules;*
- *Data Transitional Rules;*
- *Transient Data Stores.*

You will use these to prepare your Legacy Data Stores to a level consistent with the Data Quality Rules. Along the way you can expect to uncover additional Legacy Data Stores and line up some new Data Stakeholders.

STEP 1.0: STAGE INITIATION

From Stage 0 you will have a tentative list of Key Business Data Areas agreed with the programme, a first-cut catalogue of Legacy Data Stores and an accompanying (if incomplete) list of Data Stakeholders. Your project change management has all these lists firmly under control. Your data migration strategy document has been duly signed off and filed away with the programme documents and your provisional first stage plan has been approved.

You are probably still canvassing for all those additional Legacy Data Stores, but the deadline for an amnesty on disclosure is drawing near. Anyway you have a meaty list of Legacy Data Stores to kick off with and the resources are available to make a serious start.

If any of the above is not the case then either get it in place right now, or go through your normal risk mitigation procedure.

STEP 1.1: ANALYSE LEGACY DATA STORES

For each Legacy Data Store prepare a Legacy Data Store definition form. Traditional business analysis skills are required for this task:
- examining documentation, data base schemas, file formats;
- documenting business usage;
- interviewing Business Domain Experts and Data Store Owners.

In addition, there are the following new requirements:

- identifying Data Stakeholders;
- generating initial data quality assessments;
- creating the questions you will take into Step 1.3 (create first-cut System Retirement Policies).

You will find that as this task progresses your understanding of the legacy Key Business Data Areas increases, so this task feeds into Step 1.2 (update Key Business Data Area models). Similarly, updates elsewhere on the project will be reflected in updated Key Business Data Area models and the degree of fit between your Legacy Data Stores and the Key Business Data Area models will alter. This means that your data quality assessment will alter as well.

> ### Hint
>
> It is because of the close relationship between Key Business Data Areas and Legacy Data Store models that where the scale of the migration demands a large team of migration experts I tend to organize work by Key Business Data Area.
>
> Organizing resource by Key Business Data Area also, generally, has the benefit of building stronger ties between the Data Migration Analysts and their Data Stakeholders.

This is also the point at which the first decisions are taken as to which data stores to include and which to exclude from migration. Some data stores may be mandated by the project initiation document or are so obviously core to the business that they must be included.

Other data stores will appear to be so weakly derivative of data held elsewhere that they should be excluded. However, all data stores should be visited, if only briefly, and a Legacy Data Store definition form drawn up for them and placed under change control. It is the duty of a well-managed data migration project to clean up after itself and not to leave vestigial data stores in its wake. If it exists prior to migration, after migration each data store will have been:

- migrated and removed;
- left untouched; or
- removed untouched.

Take this opportunity to clear out the dross that litters too many departments. Each data store targeted for removal should have its own System Retirement Policy initiated and signed off by the Data Store Owner at this point.

Just as importantly, although it may be apparent which data stores are going to be significant to your project and which can be written off, as we saw in the worked example earlier, it is not until you have completed Stage 2 Data Preparation that you will know where all the data gaps are. Only then can you be certain that you have enough data to fill them. You may find, as you draw up your Stage 2 Data Quality Rules, perform data model comparisons and commence Data Mapping, that a data store dismissed in Stage 1 holds data in a more appropriate format. Alternatively a dismissed data store, even if not used directly, can be of use in validating or cross-referencing data items held elsewhere.

At this point also, you have not performed any formal data quality analysis, you have only the impressionistic views of the Data Stakeholders to go on. These can prove to be coloured by local preferences. The Stage 1 Data Quality Rules process may cause the project to rethink its choice of Legacy Data Store.

Finally, remember Golden Rule 2. If the data store exists it should be assumed it does so for a reason (until the Data Store Owner is convinced otherwise). Do the business the courtesy of taking their data stores seriously. Failing to place a data store on the register risks it being reintroduced later. If it has been considered and objectively rejected this will save time going over the same ground a second (and third, fourth etc) time.

> **Hint**
>
> Be aware of synonyms for data stores. The same data store can be called by a different name elsewhere in the business. Usually this is merely a historical accident but it can hint at two or more uses for the same store, which implies two or more Business Domain Experts. Whatever the reason, try to get the business to agree on a single name and record the synonym(s) on the Legacy Data Store form.

STEP 1.2: UPDATE KEY BUSINESS DATA AREA MODELS

From Stage 0 you will have received an initial decomposition of the migration problem into Key Business Data Areas. Each area may have been documented to the level of Conceptual Entity Model (or to whatever levels your choice of alternative modelling technique prescribes). If not do so now. We also need to extend the detail as we recover it from the analysis of the Legacy Data Stores. The data models we are creating here are the data models of how the legacy Key Business Data Area should be structured. We expect that individual Legacy Data Stores will conform to this model to a greater or lesser degree. The degree of conformity will be uncovered in the first iteration of Stage 1 Data Quality Rules.

Once again the level of detail we go to here is limited by time, available skills and need. Where a single corporate Legacy Data Store masters a Key Business Data Area it is unnecessary to replicate its data analysis in the documentation of the Key Business Data Area. A reference to the appropriate documentation will suffice.

> **Hint**
>
> By 'masters' I do not mean that it is the only Legacy Data Store in the Key Business Data Area, but that it is the recognized standard from which others diverge. However, bear in mind that your master data store may itself diverge, in part, from its own standards. It will need Data Quality Rules to establish its conformity to its own rules and Data Quality Rules to fix any issues uncovered.

Where there is more than one Legacy Data Store then a synthesis of their data structures will be required. The objective is to produce a model against which individual Legacy Data Stores can be compared.

> **Hint**
>
> Beware academic correctness here. We are after a reasonable standard against which local divergence can be measured. Of course it has to be a good likeness of the reality experienced by our Business Domain Experts, but it is the differences between individual Legacy Data Stores and the Key Business Data Area model that we are interested in as much as the perfection of the model itself. It is easy to confuse the means (the Key Business Data Area model) with the ends (the successful migration of business data). But that way lies the dreadful analysis vortex which can waste days (even weeks) of project time for what is an intermediary product.

STEP 1.3: CREATE FIRST-CUT SYSTEM RETIREMENT POLICIES

From the moment a Legacy Data Store is identified as a probable candidate for replacement by the new system, a System Retirement Policy should be initiated. Some data stores will be completely overtaken by new system functionality. Others will be partially overtaken. Even at this early stage it will be clear in the majority of cases where an individual Legacy Data Store sits, however there will be examples where choices will have to be made as to where the data is to be migrated from and against what it will be validated. In all cases, those data stores that are covered, even partially, by the new system should be targeted for removal and a System Retirement Policy initiated. At this stage this is a statement of requirements not a solution.

Hint

Be careful that you do not, at this point, re-import into the programme functionality that has already been scoped out of the main body of design. Although signed off by the Data Store Owner, System Retirement Policies should be reviewed at all stages by the Programme Expert responsible for this Key Business Data Area.

STEP 1.4: CREATE DATA QUALITY RULES

By the end of Stage 1 we need our Legacy Data Stores sufficiently consistent with the legacy Key Business Data Area models to allow the project to move forward to the second stage of data preparation. The Legacy Data Stores must be prepared to a known degree of divergence with the legacy Key Business Data Area models so that there are no nasty surprises later. There will therefore be two types of Data Quality Rule at this point. The first measures the degree of conformity to our expressed rules. The second takes steps to fix problems uncovered. Although it is often easier to fix data *in situ* (it reduces the need for Data Transitional Rules), we need to judge whether we are fixing problems that will benefit us when we get to Stage 2 and beyond. On the other hand, given that in most programmes the new system analysis and development stream is late delivering a full functional specification, there is usually waiting time that is best utilized fixing problems that may trip us up downstream.

Hint

In practice if we find the correct Business Domain Experts they will know the major data issues the business faces and how to fix them. In that case one Data Quality Rules document can have both types of rule in it.

However you do it, though, all Data Quality Rules have to be tested, even those that you are assured are

> rigorously enforced. Better to waste a bit of energy in reassurance now than compromise the project later.
>
> And all Data Quality Rules, even 'fix it' ones need a metrics Data Quality Rule to measure their success. Don't forget Golden Rule 4!

Data Quality Rules come in one of three categories:

- **Internal consistency:** The most significant check at this stage. Each Data Store is checked to ascertain how far it meets its own rules.
- **Model consistency:** Checks should be made against the legacy Key Business Data Area model to check for its consistency.
- **Reality Check:** It may be apparent even at this point that there are differences between what is held in the data store and the existent reality it is intended to represent.

> **Hint**
>
> I am not suggesting here that all data stores can be exhaustively re-audited against the items they are intended to represent. This is often impractical, but concrete evidence must be sought to grade the degree of fit between the data and the things it represents. It is essential that you build relationships with the Business Domain Experts and seek their advice on how to produce the metrics, the amount of known discrepancy there is and which discrepancies are most significant. Don't forget Golden Rules 1 and 2!

STEP 1.5: ENACT DATA QUALITY RULES

For the first iteration of Data Quality Rules we are interested in establishing the size of the problem or the degree of consistency with the rules. In the second iteration we are going to fix those problems. As indicated above, where there is a clearly established knowledge of a data quality problem then the two actions can be planned and documented within a single Data Quality Rules document. Where this happens, measurement must still precede data quality enhancement activity. Remember Golden Rule 4!

Data quality enhancement is generally an intensely business-dependent activity. In other words, it places an inordinate burden on the front-line users of Legacy Data Stores. You will, in every migration exercise I have ever been involved with, be time-limited by the bigger programme plan. The key user personnel may not be sufficiently available in the required time frame. Compromises will have to be made. The Data Stakeholders must make these decisions and not the data migration project. Because this is Stage 1 data cleansing and we are operating in parallel with new system design, generally the Programme Experts will not be fully up to speed with their precise requirements and will also be heavily committed to development roles.

This is your big opportunity to really add value to the programme and the business, gain kudos with your business partners and create that business ownership of the data migration project that you so need if you are to succeed. Take advantage of this opportunity to build your virtual team, in common cause with your business allies.

Get the Data Store Owners, Business Domain Experts and other Data Stakeholders as involved as possible in finding a solution. Make it a joint business problem.

You may suggest some, or all, of the following compromises in lieu of a full cleanse:

- Postpone some data cleansing activities until Stage 2 Data Preparation.

> **Hint**
>
> If the Data Store Owners are made aware of the issues and options ahead of time there is a greater chance that they may be able to make the right resources available. Too often we only turn to the business when time is pressing and our need is urgent.

- Prioritize those activities that can be completed within the timescale and with the resources available.

- Cleanse data to a known degree of conformity but short of perfection (this is based on the old 80:20 principle that the first 80% of any task can be completed with the first 20% of effort and things get progressively harder from then on. It also aligns with Golden Rule 3).

- Go live with the existing data problems until a new, stand-alone, data cleansing project is funded.

- Go live with the existing data problems but put business procedures in place that will clean the data over time.

> **Anecdote**
>
> I was working for a regional water utility where it was not feasible to resurvey all their pumps to get the correct model details. These details were needed because the new system allowed scheduling maintenance to

> be differentiated based on model type not just on time since last visit. We altered the work process so that the engineer reported the model type back as well as the other details on their time sheet. A temporary dummy model type was placed against the pumps at data load time. Within one maintenance cycle we could report that better than 95% of pumps had been inspected and a corrected model type submitted.

- Go live with the existing data problems and live with them as was done previously. (Remember Golden Rule 3.)

Whichever solution the Data Store Owners choose, it has to be their choice. The most significant discussions you will have are often around prioritizing data cleansing activities. Gain the Data Store Owners' acceptance of Golden Rule 3 and you will now be having what I would call an adult discussion about realistic choices taken in the light of known, measurable, data quality issues.

DATA TRANSITIONAL RULES

When data cleansing is taking place, whether it is *in situ* or in a Transient Data Store, you must consider creating Data Transitional Rules. The business world moves on, and any data snapshot will be ageing from the moment it is taken.

Any significant change to operating procedures can only be sanctioned by someone at Data Store Owner level, lower level changes might be within the initiative of a Business Domain Expert. Either way they must be specified by the Data Store Owner or Business Domain Expert and included in the Data Quality Rules document. Your role as Data Migration Analyst is to be aware of the need for Data Transitional Rules and to facilitate their development and possibly oversee their implementation.

TRANSIENT DATA STORES

It may be that data can only be cleansed by removing it from source, manipulating it externally then be reloading it back into the Legacy Data Store. Within Stage 1 Data Preparation this degree of development is to be resisted on any but the simplest data store. You will probably not have the time or knowledge to analyse the complete impact of whole scale unload–load activities. This is, after all, a data store earmarked for retirement. Ask yourself: if data cleansing has to take place externally can this be done safely? Can it wait until Stage 2 Data Preparation? Can the cleansed data be held until Stage 3 then loaded straight into the new system?

Transient Data Stores can also be used to create cross reference tables or for splitting composite data items where there is a disparity between the

Key Business Data Area model and the Legacy Data Store model. These are all legitimate uses of Transient Data Stores but need they be created now, or can they be planned now but created and managed in Stage 2?

USE OF RECURSION

There will be recursion at this stage around the following steps:

- Analysing Legacy Data Stores and update Key Business Area models. These two steps sit side by side and should always be performed in tandem.

- Creating Data Quality Rules and enact Data Quality Rules. There will be at least two iteration cycles around these two steps. The first pass establishes the Data Quality Rules and tests them against the data, the second pass uses the output from the first to establish and enact data cleansing rules. But testing data quality of itself will often throw up additional problems, for which new rules will need to be written.

- Testing Data Quality Rules will often uncover further Legacy Data Stores and these will lead to another Stage 1 cycle.

- Testing Data Quality Rules will often lead the project to question the choice of target Legacy Data Store, this in turn should be reflected in the Legacy Data Store documentation and so leads to a return to analysing Legacy Data Stores and updating Key Business Data Area models. It may have an impact on the System Retirement Policy for that data store.

STAGE 1 CLOSEDOWN

At the end of this stage the following should be available to be handed over to the next stage.

- A complete list of legacy Key Business Data Areas documented to logical data model detail.

- A complete list of Legacy Data Stores, documented and under change control. Each will be assigned to one or more Key Business Data Area. Each will have at least an impressionistic data quality assessment. The list will be divided into: those data stores that will almost certainly be used in the migration process; those that may have some item either directly or in validation that is of interest to the next two stages; and those that will probably take no further part in the project.

- A comprehensive list of Data Stakeholders will be available. Each Legacy Data Store will have a Data Store Owner and Business Domain Expert assigned to it. The other Data Stakeholder roles will be listed as appropriate.

- Completed and part-completed Data Quality Rules documents and tasks. All Legacy Data Stores that are likely to be targeted in the remainder of the data migration project will have at least one Data Quality Rules document that will have measured the store's accuracy.

- Completed and signed off Stage 1 System Retirement Policies. These will be completed for each Legacy Data Store that is a candidate for retirement. At this point they are little more than a list of requirements that must be met for the store to be successfully retired.

STAGE 1 PROJECT CONTROLS

This is the most iterative section of the data migration project. This stage will not follow the traditional waterfall 'Analyse – Design – Build' steps of a standard development project. As project manager you will be controlling this section of the project by:

- time slicing;
- creating work packages to analyse Key Business Areas;
- predicting the number and complexity of Data Quality Rules activities from the number of Legacy Data Stores identified, and then the impressionistic data quality assessments contained within them;
- managing each Data Quality Rule (once they have all been created) as a mini-project in its own right – but be aware that, given the significant business involvement, the elapsed time will exceed the resource time;
- being prepared to allow some Data Quality Rules activities to 'overflow' into Stage 2 Data Preparation, but only do this where the task is, of necessity, of long duration and is of major importance to the business.

> **Hint**
>
> I personally like tidy planning and do not allow tasks to overflow from one stage to another on my project plans. If necessary I will terminate the task within one stage and recommence it within the next. This may seem pedantic but it challenges the task's reasons for overflowing and means that there is a clear break point between stages where a major replanning exercise takes place.

For most of Stage 1 and Stage 2, Data Quality Rules will be the project's key controlling activities. Each should be a little plan in its own right, with its own deliverables. As in any good project planning exercise, try to keep inter-plan contentions to a minimum. If two or more Data Quality Rules of the same type (ie two investigatory or two cleansing Data Quality Rules) use the same resources, consider putting them together into a single document. It is usually more efficient to fix or investigate two sets of data issues in one pass than to attempt them sequentially. One skilled Business Domain Expert can as easily check two fields on a target record as one if they are given the appropriate tools. But once again, be driven by the advice of your Key Stakeholders. At least by putting both Data Quality Rules into the one document they can be prioritized.

Encouraging a high degree of autonomy in Data Quality Rules means that they can be managed in parallel. There is no reason why one Key Business Data Area cannot be completed before another is started, nor is there any reason why they cannot be worked on at the same time.

The time it takes documenting Key Business Data Areas is dependent on the degree of skill in the modelling technique you have, the complexity of the technique, the complexity of the Key Business Data Area and the availability of any previous analysis. This is why I stick to simple techniques that are quick to teach and easy to perform without complex software. Data modelling is a standard industry task so you should be able to estimate based on local experience. Remember initially we only want it to be good enough to move on. Although they are placed under change control, these are intermediary deliverables and are not to be signed off. It is the Data Quality Rules that are singed off.

To calculate the effort required to analyse Legacy Data Stores in Stage 1, I usually work to a rule of thumb of three days' effort per Legacy Data Store to create the initial Legacy Data Store documents and get them signed off. This is of course based on there being a number (greater than 20) of Legacy Data Stores so that the more complex are averaged out with the more simple. And please note this is effort, not elapsed time. Tracking down a Data Store Owner and getting a signature on paper can take – well, again, you will know your own environment! After the first few your estimating will get better, so make sure you take time to review these metrics and replan.

To calculate an estimate of the effort required in Stage 1 for Data Quality Rules activity take the number of Legacy Data Stores identified plus an estimate for the number that will come out later (bearing in mind that it is usually the smaller, less complex data stores that come out last). Review the assumptions about the quality of the data in the Legacy Data Stores and match this to the Key Business Data Area rules to produce an estimate for the number of Data Quality Rules that will need to be produced. This will tell you how many mini-plans you will be tracking. As to the effort and elapsed time for each Data Quality Rule this will only be known for certain once the rule has been written, but experience should guide you as to the amount of time and effort involved. This is one reason I favour an iterative approach – with every iteration your estimating skills are better honed.

Hint

Normally the programme time line is fixed, which inverts the normal planning paradigm. If time is fixed then only quality, resources or quantity can change. This is the moment to ask your key Data Stakeholders to prioritize your activities. Find out from the Data Store Owners how many Business Domain Experts they can commit to the project and for how long. Remember Golden Rule 1 and Golden Rule 3; it is your job to balance the requirements of the programme expressed via the Programme Experts with the constraints imposed on the enterprise as expressed by the other key Data Stakeholders. The Programme Experts have their drivers in terms of when they need the data to be in a certain state. The question then is how far can we go to meet them, and by 'we' I mean the whole virtual team of Data Stakeholders. Expect to go round the loop a few times getting an agreed plan.

Chapter review

At this point in the project you will have:
- *built a virtual team linking business and project;*
- *discovered and analysed the project's Legacy Data Stores;*
- *discovered and documented Data Stakeholders;*
- *synthesized a single data model for each Key Business Data Area;*
- *created and enacted Data Quality Rules that align the Legacy Data Stores to a known degree of conformity within themselves, within the Key Business Data Areas and with the real world of the business;*
- *initiated System Retirement Policies.*

11 Stage 2 Data Preparation

In this chapter you will be:
- *introducing the new system model;*
- *creating Stage 2 Data Quality Rules;*
- *creating extract, transform and load definitions;*
- *enhancing System Retirement Policies;*
- *optionally creating Data Transitional Rules;*
- *optionally creating Transient Data Stores.*

You will use these to prepare your data migration design.

STEP 2.0: STAGE INITIATION

From Stage 1 you will have a comprehensive list of Key Business Data Areas agreed with the programme, a catalogue of Legacy Data Stores and an accompanying list of Data Stakeholders. Each Legacy Data Store will have been analysed and categorized as a:

- target Legacy Data Store that will almost certainly have data migrated from it;
- Legacy Data Store that may have some item either directly or in validation that may be of interest or;
- Legacy Data Store that will probably take no further part in the project.

Your project change management has all these lists firmly under control.

You may still have some Stage 1 Data Quality Rule work ongoing, with the linked possibility of Transient Data Stores and Data Transitional Rules in operation.

Finally and most significantly, you cannot start this stage until you have a clear view of the new system design. This has to be a model in a format compatible with your Legacy Data Store and Key Business Data Area models. It may be that the implementation method of your programme does not routinely deliver such a model. This should have been sorted out in the data migration strategy document and an allowance for building such a model put into the programme plan.

Hint

When projects are running late or where there is a high degree of modularization in the new system, there may be pressure to commence this phase before a full design is available for the whole of the new system. This is possible, but involves a severe risk of rework becoming necessary. Getting the user population to rework data preparation they have already carried out is very unpopular, so resist moving forward unless you are assured that the tentative design you are working to is unlikely to alter. Make sure that your change control procedures are robust and any changes to the new system will be communicated to you and reflected in the new system data model. Partitioning of the programme into Key Business Data Areas that are meaningful both to the legacy and to the new system environment helps hugely to contain the impact of late changes.

Where Stage 1 Data Quality Rules have revealed that there is an external mismatch between data store and reality, re-auditing will be low risk. It is probably something that will have to be done come what may.

Creation of extract, transform and load definitions internal to the data migration project team is also possible because – hey, you're a project person and as such used to being messed about by late design changes and can work within the confines of change control.

But be careful to explain the risks to and protect your key Data Stakeholders from change. You have spent too much time and energy building relationships to allow them to get spoilt now.

If any of the above is not the case, then either get it in place right now, or go through your normal risk mitigation procedure.

Now is the time to firm up your Stage 2 plan and get it approved.

STEP 2.1: NOMINATE CANDIDATE LEGACY DATA STORES

We now have:

- the new system design;
- Legacy Data Store definition forms;
- legacy Key Business Data Area models;
- Stage 1 Data Quality Rules documents showing the fit between Legacy Data Stores and the various legacy models;
- System Retirement Policies.

From these we need to make comparisons, find the data gaps and the best fits between legacy data, new system data requirements and Legacy Data Store retention requirements.

So how are we going to make sense of all of this and bring the enterprise along with us?

I suggest the following, but the way you will proceed in practice will depend on which of the above products are carrying the most weight and the most risk. Do the System Retirement Policies point one way but the Data Quality Rules point another? Is the new system data model a better match for one Legacy Data Store than another?

The important thing is that as skilled information technologists we must have all the information we need plus mechanisms for resolving these issues. By following the principles and the practices advocated in this book so far, then we do!

I normally start with desktop activities before involving the other Data Stakeholders. I familiarise myself with the new system data models, then bring in the Programme Experts and Technical Data Experts to discuss design options. When we have an Aunt Sally set of solutions I approach the other Data Stakeholders for confirmation. I do this is because I think there are technical appraisals and decisions that are best taken prior to consulting with the enterprise. However, this can change on a case-by-case basis depending on the quality of the handover from the new system designers, the technical sophistication of the Business Domain Experts and the method by which the new system design was arrived at. The same deliverables from Stage 1 are used but the sequence of tasks and personnel involved may change.

In whichever order we consult with the Data Stakeholders, the candidate Legacy Data Stores have to be agreed by all the relevant Data Stakeholders.

Step 2.1.1 gap analysis

In this step we compare legacy Key Business Data Area models to the new system data models. I usually choose to start my investigation at the Conceptual Entity Model level and work my way down. This is because finding the big gaps between legacy Key Business Data Area and new system data structures are more likely to drive out the bigger pieces of work earlier, rather than finding out the problems at a field-by-field level.

Anecdote

You will be surprised at how many projects do start to work at a field-by-field level mapping exercise. Of course when the big navigation problems arrive they then have to backtrack through the Legacy Data Stores and, usually in a tearing hurry, re-engineer the deliverables.

> ### Hint
>
> I also advocate a 'heads up' approach to data migration projects. Stay involved with the rest of the programme team and try to spot issues early. Try to get them to deliver data models to you on a Key Business Data Area basis at draft stage so that you are aware in advance and can have discussions with the other Data Stakeholders. This is one reason why proximity is important. These are the sorts of issues that can be chatted about in coffee machine conversations. Never underestimate the importance of the informal.

The key techniques here are access path analysis to identify access gaps, data structure analysis to identify data structure problems, and data gap analysis to identify missing data items.

Access gaps

Remember that for data migration an access path has only to be tenable – it does not have to be efficient or elegant. We need only establish connections to allow data to be loaded into the new system. These designs are not permanent and are going to be thrown away once the migration is over. Stage 3 Build, Test and Go Live will resolve performance issues.

> ### Hint
>
> The requirement for speed of performance is often overstated in data migration projects. I had much rather that the migration be right than efficient. It may take 18 months to get data from its raw state in the Legacy Data Stores to the point where migration can occur. Shaving minutes off the run time for the final load programs saves next to nothing compared with the overall effort. It is more important to be clear about the rules in the System Retirement Policies, the limits on down time and on having mitigating Data Transitional Rules in place. I find that by making the enterprise part owners of the solution along with the technicians, 'impossibly' long run times suddenly become possible.

Data structure problems

These are the problems that require the best grasp of data modelling principles. The new system may have its own nomenclature so problems of synonym and homonym abound.

Synonyms and homonyms

Homonym – two words that are spelt or pronounced the same way but have a different meaning. In a business context the word 'account' will mean something different to a salesman and an accountant.

Synonym – two words that are spelt differently but have the same meaning. In our example the terms 'equipment' and 'machine' can mean the same thing.

Synonyms and homonyms are one of the bugbears of a migration analyst's life.

You need to be confident in your ability to match structures that do not, on the face of it, appear the same and to be able to discern differences in data structures that appear similar. But do not worry. Every assumption will be tested as you work down the data structures so anything you missed will be revealed later. It just helps to spot issues early then you will not have to back track later to resolve them.

Data gaps

Because at this point you are dealing with data at the conceptual entity level, it will not be minor fields that are missing but whole entities. Although this is a major programme issue, it is so large and so obvious that it is unlikely to have escaped the attention of anyone involved with the programme. Thought will probably already have been given to it. Indeed, the creation of a repository for a new conceptual entity is often the principal driver for new system development – the enterprise is engaged in activity it has never carried out before and so needs new tools and concepts. Your key Data Stakeholders, especially the Data Store Owners, will be awaiting your solution to the problem of the missing entity. If you have managed Stage 1 appropriately they will also be ready with at least one proposed solution.

Anecdote

I have worked on a number of projects where from the initial conversation onwards the Programme Board is clearly focussed on the 'missing' data as if it were the only migration issue. Do not allow yourself to be dragged into this group-think. You still need to carry out all the other data migration steps because the overlooked are just as capable of tripping you up as the obvious. File it away for Stage 2 Data Preparation. It may even be politically expedient to draw up a skeleton Data Quality Rules document – it is never too early to get the Data Stakeholders involved in the solution. However, you cannot resolve it until Stage 1 Data Preparation, for the Key Business Data Area where this Legacy Data Store resides, at least, is completed.

Step 2.1.2: record and fill data gaps

If we characterize all these missing data issues as data gaps for shorthand, the next steps can be defined once, although as you proceed through your Stage 2 Data Quality Rules processes you will have to structure the solution to them slightly differently.

Data gaps should be recorded and become the subject of Data Quality Rules exercises in their own right. Record them in the Data Quality Rules register and process them through that mechanism. Each data gap will generate two Data Quality Rules – one for measurement and one to fix it (even if the fix is to live with the anomaly).

> **Hint**
>
> This is the point where a Legacy Data Store previously discarded as derivative or less than optimal can come into its own. Where there is an access step missing, review the other Legacy Data Store definitions within that Key Business Data Area. Is there one that will fill that gap for you? Where data structure problems appear, see if the problem has been solved already in some obscure database. Where a conceptual entity is missing – well, it can happen that someone somewhere has recorded it already, but it is unlikely that this will not have been recognized prior to you initiating this stage.

If there is a Legacy Data Store to help you out, you will still need to create a Data Quality Rule to check the degree to which this resolves the issue. It is unlikely that it will have been checked in Stage 1. Does the Legacy Data Store fill the data gap in every instance or only a given percentage of the time? In what circumstances does it not resolve the issue? What steps can be taken to make it resolve the issue? How accurately does this Legacy Data Store reflect existent reality? All these questions need to be raised by looking at the Legacy Data Store definition and associated Stage 1 Data Quality Rules and probably going back to the Legacy Data Store itself. From this, Stage 2 Data Quality Rules will be generated.

If there is no Legacy Data Store that can fill the data gap then a Data Quality Rule to resolve the issue is inevitable. It is also extremely likely that a Transient Data Store will also be required.

Step 2.1.3: Legacy Data Store selection

Having initiated comparisons at the top level, which will, of themselves, influence the selection process, it is now time to progress down the levels to the individual Legacy Data Store definitions. You have your Conceptual Entity Models, you know the data content and quality of the data stores for each Key Business Data Area. Make your selection and proceed to create the draft extract, transform and load definitions. On very large system migrations these should be in outline only, not necessarily field by field. Simply show, for each group of data items, the likely source of data. Get agreement between the Data Stakeholders then move down a layer to a field-by-field mapping.

Step 2.1.4: prepare for review of draft deliverables

You need to get your draft suggestions in front of the Data Stakeholders as soon as possible to retain their ownership of the solution. Therefore as soon as the results of your desktop activities are available they need to be formally reviewed by the key Data Stakeholders.

> **Hint**
>
> I suggest a maximum of two weeks' elapsed time from getting the formal handover of the finished new system design to holding your first Stage 2 Data Quality Rules facilitated meetings. It is imperative that you keep the momentum up.

These reviews should take the form of Data Quality Rules meetings. The Data Stakeholders will be familiar by now with the format and where additional data gap or proof of concept work is required this can be captured in a form with which everyone is familiar.

You need to present the output from 2.1.1, 2.1.2 and 2.1.3 for confirmation and resolution by the Data Stakeholders who will own the solution. These intermediary deliverables are only stepping stones to the final Data Quality Rules, System Retirement Policies and extract, transform and load definitions that will emerge from the Data Quality Rules process. They therefore only need to be 'good enough' for the purpose, not perfectly polished. They should be more like briefing documents than system specifications.

However, the combination of these documents is greater than the sum of the parts. Give yourself planned time to put them together into suitable work packages for discussion at your Stage 2 Data Quality Rules meetings.

There is no hard and fast rule for how to combine items into these work packages, but the following factors should be considered:

- **Resources:** Which items need which combination of human and technical resources (especially Data Stakeholders) to resolve? When are they going to be available?

- **Duration:** Ideally, each Data Quality Rules generation meeting should not take longer than one day. If there is a controversial item it may be worth putting it on its own.

- **Proximity:** Group items together for consideration if they affect the same area within the organization.
- **Consequential impact:** Where a mapping suggestion will have an impact on a retirement policy etc, then putting that group together will be beneficial.

Get your documents, slides and presentations together, notify your Data Stakeholders and prepare for the most intense set of activities of the data migration project!

Planning

This step is one of the key planning steps. By the end of this step the shape of the remainder of Stage 2 and therefore Stage 3 will be clear:

- the number, duration and complexity of Data Quality Rules;
- the probable number of Transient Data Stores;
- the probable number and complexity and data repositories that will be needed for System Retirement Policies;
- the number of System Retirement Policies;
- the complexity of the extract, transform and load activities, and from that the coding and testing etc.

From these metrics a good estimate of the scale of the remainder of the project can be drawn.

> **Hint**
>
> **Make allowance in your plan for recursion. From what you know about the strength of the underlying assumptions, how many of the suggested solutions will be shown by the Data Quality Rules process to be untenable and thus demand reworking?**

STEP 2.2: CREATE STAGE 2 DATA QUALITY RULES

There are several types of Stage 2 Data Quality Rules exercises:

- data gap;
- data quality;
- extract, transform and load definition.

Each should be approached in the same generic manner.

- Investigate, in consultation with key Data Stakeholders.
- Optionally propose a 'straw man' solution.
- Put the issue in front of the appropriate Data Stakeholders.

- Provide a venue where a solution can be thrashed out.
- Prototype and document the solution.
- Ensure that each solution (other than 'live with it') has accompanying metrics.
- Work through the solution until the metrics of completion are reached or a new Data Quality Rules exercise is required.

Iteration

Because you will have prepared the Legacy Data Stores to a known degree of conformance with the legacy models, there should be fewer data quality iterations than in Stage 1. However, you must plan for discovering discrepancies that are only revealed when the new system design is brought to bear on the Legacy Data Stores.

I cannot prescribe in this book how much iteration you should be planning for. If the new system Key Business Data Area model and the legacy models are a good match, you may find that all that is needed is limited data manipulation and enhancement. On the other hand, the introduction of the new system model, especially if there has been any business process re-engineering involved, may be at such variance to the legacy model that two passes will be needed: a first-pass quantification Data Quality Rules exercise to establish if data of the required quality is present then a second-pass to prepare the data for migration.

Stage 2 consistency checks

For Stage 2 Data Preparation:

- **Internal consistency:** This is the least significant check at this stage. Each data store will have been checked at Stage 1 for internal consistency albeit in a cursory manner for those data stores we just 'knew' we were not going to use. Well, this is the point where we find out if we made the right call!

- **External consistency:** We know from Stage 1 to what degree each data store diverges from the legacy Key Business Data Area model. By comparing the legacy Key Business Data Area model with the new system data model we will know where the data structural gaps lie and therefore how far the target data store data structure diverges from the new system data structure.

- **Reality Check:** There will be two types of Reality Check problem:

  1. Where there was an existing problem with Legacy Data Store data quality. This will have been quantified in the Data Quality Rules from Stage 1, but for reasons of time or because the new design could not be second-guessed, you choose to postpone data cleansing until Stage 2. You have to resolve with your Data

Stakeholders why, if the previous data was poor but still ran the enterprise, you need to enhance data quality and by how much. The data migration project team does not have the knowledge and should not take on the responsibility to decide this. It will become an issue between the Data Store Owners, the Business Domain Experts and the Programme Experts. The Audit and Regulation Experts and the Technical Data Experts may also want to contribute. Organize a forum where it can be discussed by the experts and settled. Record the results in a Data Quality Rules document.

2. Where entirely new data is required for the new system that has never been collected by the business before, this almost always requires the building of a Transient Data Store.

Anecdote

This occurs less often than we might think. Usually it hints at the existence of a hidden data store, maybe a local one that has not previously been automated. Find out from your Business Domain Experts. I have been involved more often with data take on in situations where the level of granularity required by the new system was at a lower level of detail than was recorded by the Legacy Data Stores, than I have with genuinely new data.

Extract, transform and load Data Quality Rules meetings

Extract, transform and load definition is messy. On the one hand there are the Business Domain Experts. They know the value of the data in each field and its meaning to them. On the other hand are the Legacy Data Store Technical Data Experts. They know what lies 'under the hood' and is not necessarily visible to the users in terms of referential integrity constraints, ease of extraction, data formatting issues etc. Add to these the Programme Experts' demand for data of a given format and it's easy to see how in some projects the Business Domain Expert's view is squeezed out.

All of this is further complicated by the time pressures most projects are under and by the sheer size of the task of creating extract, transform and load definitions for thousands of rows. As the Data Migration Analyst it is your responsibility to make sure that the right weight is given to each party, and this will be different on a case by case basis.

Ideally one would have all three parties together perform the mapping. In practice this is not always possible. It is more often the Business Domain Experts who are most pushed for time. They are the ones, after all, for whom this is in addition to the day job. However, we do have the Legacy Data Store definition forms and the Stage 1 Data Quality Rules documents to guide the technologists.

However you manage your project, the business-side Data Stakeholders must be given final approval.

> **Hint**
>
> This is why I normally start from a conceptual entity level and work down. I get agreement to broad elements of the mappings at entity level then the technologists can go away and develop sections of detailed mappings. The business-side Data Stakeholders then formally review the suggested mappings. This review must be completed face to face in a formal meeting because typically the Business Domain Expert will not know the meaning and use of the new system data elements and you will need the technologists to explain the basis of some of their decisions. However, be on your guard for apparently technical judgements that mask personal preferences or coding expediency.

It is of the utmost importance that the extract, transform and load definitions are tested. Again, I do this by creating Data Quality Rules for the extract, transform and load definitions that quantify the degree to which the data is available, in the right format, to the right quality. Data Quality Rules provide us with a format the project understands and an accepted method of reporting and dealing with any data quality issues that are uncovered.

STEP 2.3: ENACT DATA QUALITY RULES

Although there is less likely to be a quantifying iteration than a fixing iteration, the same rules as in Stage 1 apply. Remember Golden Rule 4 and always measure before and after you act! If the introduction of the new system design requires new data to be gathered or a new relationship between existing data to be established, then you will need a quantifying Data Quality Rule before a data gathering Data Quality Rule even if you include the two in a single package.

This phase of data quality enhancement often requires a large commitment from the enterprise, especially where there is a data-gathering Data Quality Rule. Frequently the only people expert enough to carry out an audit or to gather data at the correct level of detail are the experts in the enterprise itself.

Anecdote

Working for a multinational broadcasting organization on a helpdesk project I had to oversee the gathering of information on the scattered assets that made up their desktops. Being new to data migration at the time, I farmed out the auditing of desktops to local contractors. They worked at night and the quality of the information they gathered made me think that maybe they worked in the dark. But to be fair to them the uninvolved user population made a difficult job impossible. Computers were moved during the day so that they got counted twice. There were whole floors of some buildings missed, even whole annexes. It was a nightmare. I learned from that experience that if you do not make the local Business Domain Experts (in this case probably the support engineers) own the problem you are likely to come a cropper. And I did! Now that I've told you about it you do not have to do the same! It may have been that the use of contractors would have been the chosen route in any case but it would have been done in the light of local knowledge.

This is where you will test just how well your team building in Stage 0 and Stage 1 was performed. By now they should be committed and enthused about completing the quest for adequate data. As an aside you can congratulate yourself at this point because this is typically the time, in most projects, where the project team turns to the business, for the first time and without warning, and is surprised at the frosty reception they receive. You will be met with open arms.

STEP 2.4: ENHANCE SYSTEM RETIREMENT POLICIES

Each Legacy Data Store will have a System Retirement Policy in place stating the minimum that must be done before the system is retired. You now also have the new system design. From the two you can work out the gaps where the new system design will not fulfil essential business rules for legacy data.

Hint

A warning here – it is not the responsibility of the data migration project to audit the new system design. New functionality will always differ from old in some way. That is for the Programme Experts to propose and resolve through their own mechanisms. What you have to consider is access to historical data and the processing of overhanging transactions (for Data Transitional Rules).

You must add to the System Retirement Policies, for each Legacy Data Store you are going to retire (and assume that is all of them unless the System Retirement Policy says differently), the details of those data items that are not going to be migrated. Check against the Stage 1 System Retirement Policies for the retention rules for these Data Items.

You will then enter into a period of tripartite negotiation with yourself as mediator. On one side will be the Data Store Owner and Business Domain Expert, facing them will be the Programme Expert and Technical Data Expert. You may also have a role from a data migration team perspective if the cost and effort of building stores for legacy data not migrated is going to fall on your budget.

> **Hint**
>
> There is more than a risk here that you will have two roles to play – one as facilitator and one with an interest in keeping additional new data stores to a minimum. I usually recommend appointing an independent facilitator to any workshops arranged to resolve this.

Be clear to distinguish those data items with short transaction lives that should be handled by Data Transitional Rules, and those that genuinely need a semi-permanent data store established for them.

DATA TRANSITIONAL RULES

There will be two types of Data Transitional Rules that will need to be created in Stage 2. The first is around the use of Transient Data Stores and is familiar from Stage 1.

The second will start to emerge in Stage 2 and concern how you handle transitory data that will overlap the go live period. The full technical design will not emerge until midway through Stage 3. However, with the selection of data items to migrate made, it will start becoming obvious where there is going to be a need to handle transactions raised in one Legacy Data Store that will not be completed until after that data store has been migrated. Capture these Data Transitional Rule requirements and canvass possible solutions with the interested Data Stakeholders. Forewarning them of the implication of their migration choices will increase the chance that a more achievable set of design options will be forthcoming.

TRANSIENT DATA STORES

You may have taken my earlier advice and postponed the creation of Transient Data Stores until now, even for data quality problems that are really Stage 1 problems. Well, now is the time to resurrect those Data

Quality Rules. Always check that the arrival of the new system design does not change their design. Often the new system will have enhanced business rules that should be incorporated, or it may be worthwhile to combine a genuine Stage 2 Data Preparation activity (like data gathering) in the same Transient Data Store. However, you will have had plenty of time to prototype and develop these data stores.

You will also be creating Transient Data Stores for Stage 2 Data Quality Rules. These may be for filling data gaps or for resolving data quality issues that only become apparent during low-level extract, transform and load definition.

At this point you may be becoming aware of the need for Transient Data Stores for Stage 3. This is where data needs to be exported from one or more Legacy Data Stores and manipulated externally in some way before being applied to the new system. If you have the time and resources, and the need is unequivocal, you can prototype these data stores, but concentrate on the Stage 1 and Stage 2 Transient Data Stores.

Whichever way they arise, the same caveats apply as in Stage 1 – try to avoid unload–reload activities into Legacy Data Stores and make sure you are adequately covered by Data Transitional Rules.

STAGE 2 CLOSEDOWN

At the end of this stage the following should be available to be handed over to the next stage:

- A complete list of extract, transform and load definitions, tested to a known degree of accuracy by Stage 2 Data Quality Rules.
- Completed Stage 1 and Stage 2 Data Quality Rules documents and tasks.
- Completed and signed off Stage 2 System Retirement Policies for each Legacy Data Store that is to be retired. These will have taken the legacy requirements from Stage 1 and, in the light of the new system design, be a list of requirements for Stage 3 design and build. Potential design options and Data Transitional Rules will be included where these have been canvassed.

STAGE 2 PROJECT CONTROLS

The planning for this stage should now be getting very accurate.

- The number of Legacy Data Stores will have been established and documented.
- From your background knowledge of what is going on in the bigger programme you will be aware of what your target Legacy Data Stores are likely to be.

- Data problems within the legacy Key Business Data Areas will be well documented.

- A virtual team of Data Stakeholders has been built, so compromises in squeezing the ideal amount of activity into the time available can be made.

- The virtual team will be experienced in Data Quality Rules creation and enactment. You will have metrics for how it works in your environment.

Whether you choose to adopt the traditional waterfall approach or plan for a series of time-boxed iterations (my preferred approach) is up to you.

You will have change control firmly embedded in the project so any late changes (and there will be some) or any newly discovered Legacy Data Stores can be accommodated.

It is at this stage that the new system design was introduced. Extract, transform and load definitions, enhanced System Retirement Policies and data gaps emerged. The data gaps will be the subject of Stage 2 Data Quality Rules. The data migration build specification will be documented in the extract, transform and load definition, the Data Quality Rules and the System Retirement Policies. The System Retirement Policies hold the migration timing and interdependency requirements. They also inform the programme of the Legacy Data Repositories that need to be built. The Data Quality Rules hold definitions of Transient Data Stores needed at migration time and special coding requirements that will bridge data gaps.

All this needs to be brought together into the migration strategy. Whether you see this as the first task of the next phase or the final task of this is up to you. I always like to close off all the deliverables in one stage prior to commencing the next, and so tend to close down these deliverables at the stage end, bringing together their information into a single specification. However, the creation of a single document like this at the end of a stage does tend to lead to someone somewhere (usually on the programme board) demanding that this mammoth tome be signed off. As each of its components should already be signed off this is unnecessary and can lead to interminable delay as people try to grapple with a single complex document. You become engaged in precisely the sort of vortex you were trying to avoid, so I leave it to you to decide if you are to make the specification a programme deliverable. If you do choose to go for one document then write it in such a way that all the decisions can be traced back to their documents of origin. Do not reopen discussions on settled issues.

Chapter review

At this point in the project you will have combined the new system design with the Legacy Data Store definitions and the legacy Key Business Data Area definitions to:

- *perform gap analysis;*
- *produce Stage 2 Data Quality Rules;*
- *produce tested extract, transform and load definitions;*
- *produce requirements specifications in terms of System Retirement Policies, Data Transitional Rules, data quality rules and extract, transform and load definitions.*

12 Stage 3 Build, Test and Go Live

This is the final stage of the illustrative data migration project. Here we take the data analysed and prepared in the earlier stages and produce our programs and migration plans.

STAGE 3 OVERVIEW

In this stage I shall be at my least prescriptive. As an experienced systems builder you do not need me to tell you how to control the writing of code, how to test code or how to implement and run production code. These are all standard IT activities. What this chapter does is show how these standard activities are impacted or supported by the different world that is a data migration project.

We have developed products unique to data migration in Stages 1 and 2. Here we see how they come together to create the standard inputs expected by your coding team. We will also be producing some outputs that are unique to a properly conducted data migration exercise.

STEP 3.0: STAGE INITIATION

From the previous stages you will have a controlled list of Legacy Data Stores and extract, transform and load definitions tested to a known degree of conformance to requirement. You will know the data gaps that will need to be bridged at load time and, from the System Retirement Policies, data retention requirements of legacy data that is not to be migrated.

Step 3.0.1: review ongoing activities

There may still be Data Quality Rules activity taking place that has either slipped or is still ongoing for production reasons. You will know the state of compliance of these to the Data Quality Rules metrics and will be able to plan in the delivery of these data items and make risk assessments for their late delivery.

Hint

Once again I tend to favour a clean break with previous stages. Any overhanging tasks should be reviewed and completed on the Stage 2 plan and recreated on the Stage 3 plan if their continuation is absolutely essential.

Ask your Data Stakeholders if you really need to complete late-running Data Quality Rules activity or can the enterprise live with the data quality as it is now? Stress to them the risks of late delivery and allow them to take responsibility for the stop/continue decision. This makes real to them the costs and benefits of the decision – remember Golden Rule 1. It also often has the knock-on benefit of getting a bit more pressure on the business to deliver the Data Quality Rules activities they have signed up to. It's amazing how often, when this amount of pressure is applied, that which was essential to them in Stage 2 becomes less so in Stage 3.

Step 3.0.2: create stage plan

From the Stage 2 products a tight plan can be drawn up for delivering the final stage as outlined below.

Although there are a series of generic steps, these can proceed in parallel for different Key Business Data Areas. There should be no surprises in store for you, and even final sign-off should be easy, but spend the time now to get that detailed plan agreed with the rest of the programme.

Hint

Do not confuse the plan for developing the physical design with the plan for the migration itself. This will be a deliverable of the physical design. The Step 3.0.2 deliverable is a plan for delivering a plan (amongst other things). To prevent confusion I prefer to refer to those crucial few weeks of frantic activity as old systems are closed down and new ones initiated as the system migration 'timetable' as opposed to 'plan'.

STEP 3.1: PHYSICAL DESIGN OF MIGRATION

The inputs for this process are

- the Legacy Data Stores definitions qualified to a level of measured consistency by the Data Quality Rules;

- the extract, transform and load definitions;
- possibly Transient Data Stores created in Stage 2 that hold data gap bridging information;
- data gap definitions from Stage 2 and embedded in Data Quality Rules documents that were judged best resolved within the Stage 3 Build, Test and Go Live;
- Stage 2 System Retirement Policies – the physical design must be consistent with the contents of the relevant System Retirement Policies.

> **Hint**
>
> **Even though we have done all we can to reduce the risk of our design not working, there is still the possibility that at this point something horrible emerges. Some previously unknown feature of the new system perhaps. Well, this is where the close relationship you have built up with the Data Stakeholders comes in. This is where you save the project with a quick phone call to your contacts in the enterprise asking, 'What are *we* going to do about... '.**

Out of the design will come a system migration design specification. This will have four or possibly five components:

- the data migration timetable with Check Points;
- the Data Migration Technical Specification;
- the non-functional specification (where this is not covered elsewhere)
- the Stage 3 System Retirement Policies (with Data Transitional Rules as required);
- the Fallback plan.

These should be seen as a single composite deliverable (partitioned by Key Business Data Area to make creation easier if necessary). There will be different signatories for different aspects but the whole must be internally consistent.

Data migration timetable

Develop your timetable top down. Start by reviewing the Stage 2 System Retirement Policies. From these you will be able to determine the Windows of Opportunity and the business constraints that you must support.

Anecdote

I have rarely had the liberty of deciding when the Window of Opportunity should be. In large projects it is normally understood across the enterprise when the time slots available for large-scale data migration occur.

You will also find the audit trail and control points you will be expected to honour in the System Retirement Policies. You should liaise with the Business Domain Experts and the Data Store Owners to create a meaningful sequence.

From the Programme Experts you will have gathered the programme constraints that must be met. A quick look at the program specifications being developed in this step will give you some idea of the run times that you can hope for.

Bring this all together for a first-cut timetable but be prepared to rework it when the programs have been written and tested and you have more accurate run times to work with. It is here that you will be expected to express the sequencing and timing rules.

Hint

This is where you find that the physical and business constraints conflict. Once again, remember Golden Rule 1. Bring together the appropriate Data Stakeholders (Data Store Owner, Programme Expert and Technical Data Expert) and facilitate the process of reaching an agreement. Support the facilitation with programming and other technical experts so that the solution is technically sound, but do not allow the technical to take the lead. Out of this cycle of activity new Data Transitional Rules and amendments to System Retirement Policies can be expected, as well as amendments to program specifications and the data migration timetable. Capturing and signing off changes to user facing documents is just as important as capturing changes to technical documents.

Data Migration Technical Specification

It is not possible in this book to specify what this document will look like. Each project will have its own standards depending on local design constraints and tools.

> **Hint**
>
> Some enterprises favour a single, physical 'door stopper' of a document. Personally I prefer a library of discrete documents that go to make up a single design. It makes version control easier – you do not have to issue a whole document for each small change. It will also map onto the planning process where different programmers can be assigned to build and test discrete areas of the build.

The design document should be good enough to hand on to the system builder who will be able to code from its contents.

It should include:

- program specifications for load programs;
- program specifications for any Transient Data Stores needed during migration itself;
- technical specifications for changes to Legacy Data Stores to allow for retention of historical legacy data or the creation of new repositories. (Only, of course, where this falls under the remit of the data migration project.)

Load program specifications

As the author I do not have the temerity to presume to instruct you, the reader, on what a program specification should look like. I am assuming that you have your own standards, which in any case will be specific to the technologically employed. What I will do here is show how the deliverables specific to this approach should be used to produce program specifications.

I am also using the term 'program specification' to cover all the scripting, sorting, merging, utilizing of extract and other utilities and general technical activity that needs to be specified at this stage. It is not possible for a generic approach like this to know what combination of technical tools you will have available to you but I do know that from the outputs of Stage 2 you will have all the raw materials your technical designers need.

The extract, transform and load definitions from Stage 2 are the backbone. These will be developed to the level of programmable instructions taking account of the order of precedence outlined in the data migration timetable. The Programme and Technical Data Experts should be involved with the design and sign it off as being tenable from their perspective. The load technology being developed should take account of the validation required by the new system Key Business Area Data model, tempered by the output of the Data Quality Rules.

Transient Data Store specifications

I have only included a separate heading for these because, unlike the other technical activities above, they may need to be operated by the end users and therefore the Business Domain Experts and the Data Store Owners need to have some involvement.

> **Hint**
>
> **If there is a need for end user data manipulation at data migration load time then it will almost certainly have been recognized in Stage 2 gap analysis but have been postponed for design or other reasons. The key Data Stakeholders will have been party to the Data Quality Rules activities that generated these design solutions so will be prepared for the call on their time.**

If the Transient Data Stores are not going to be visible to people outside of the programme then treat them as part of the program specification above. If the only impact on the enterprise will be additional Data Transitional Rules to allow for transactional data to be stored, perhaps offline, for a short time then make sure the relevant System Retirement Policies are updated. The Data Store Owner and Business Domain Expert will then not need to be involved in the design and sign off of the Transient Data Store program specification but will sign off its impact via the System Retirement Policy, which is the user-facing view of the migration.

Legacy Data Store change specifications and new Legacy Data Store specifications

This is an area difficult to prejudge in a generic approach like the one in this book:

- Each site will have its own set of procedures for amending existing production systems or implementing new production systems.
- There are often other reasons for amending legacy production systems within the wider programme of which the data migration project is a part and the two sets of requirements get merged.
- Some of the amendments will have been foreseen and allowed for in the new system design from the programme.

Whichever way you find that you have to tackle them in your project, the results in the technical specifications must match the requirements and solution descriptions in the System Retirement Policies. It is the System Retirement Policies that are the sign-off from a user perspective. How you are going to interact with the rest of the programme and the enterprise in which you find yourself should have been detailed in the data migration strategy document delivered in Stage 0.

And do not forget that any long-lasting changes to operating procedures necessitated by changes to existing systems or the creation of new systems are not to be confused with Data Transitional Rules that exist only for the duration of the handover from old to new system environment. Long-lasting changes must be embedded into the operating procedures of the enterprise. Again, how this handover to the other work streams in the programme is achieved should have been agreed in the data migration strategy.

Fallback specification

The Fallback specification will be based on the System Retirement Policies, the data migration timetable and the Data Migration Technical Specification.

From the System Retirement Policies will come the imperatives that must be fulfilled for the enterprise functions to continue in the event of a failure in the go live processes. The control breaks will have been captured in the data migration timetable. This is where you express the Fallback model you are adopting under each possible failure circumstance. The Data Migration Technical Specification will tell you how the process of upload is going to be implemented physically and this has an impact on the unload program designs.

It may have its own load program specifications to perform extract, transform and load in reverse. There may be some iteration between the design of the Data Migration Technical Specification and the data migration timetable where Fallback requirements need an extended audit trail. This extended audit trail will need Transient Data Stores defined for it.

Non-functional specification

This document specifies all those physical aspects of the migration that are not directly related to programming change. I have indicated that this is an optional document because it is often not part of the migration team's responsibility to specify the servers, databases or network capability of the migration platform. A separate, system go live co-ordinating work stream often covers this. However, you will be expected to contribute data sizing information and probably some of the physical Legacy Data Store information (location, access etc) that you will have gathered in the Legacy Data Store forms.

Even where there is a responsibility on the data migration workstream to specify the hardware, software and physical environment (desks, access to buildings, commissariat factors) that they require, these are usually covered in the Data Migration Technical Specification, the go live timetable and the System Retirement Policies. However sometimes it is mandatory for this information to be gathered into a single document and it is often expedient to do so for the sake of clarity often as a useful step on the way to creating the data migration timetable. It is for you to decide in the light of the complexity of your migration environment and the degree of novel activity that your System Data Migration Technical Specification creates whether it is necessary to draw all this information together in one document. The advantages are that it provides one resource for all these essential issues. The disadvantage is that you then have to keep this document in step with the source documents.

> **Hint**
>
> I normally do draw all the non-functional features together from the various sources into one place because it makes administration and planning easier. I resist making it a signed-off project deliverable, however, because its disparate nature makes it a difficult document to get signed off and there is no point in producing a deliverable that cannot be delivered!

Stage 3 System Retirement Policies

System Retirement Policies will have been developed throughout Stage 1 and Stage 2. At each stage they will have been signed off. Now is the time for the final sign-off that precedes migration. As I have outlined above, Stage 3 System Retirement Policies should be developed in tandem with the physical design. Where design or programme constraints dictate that System Retirement Policy objectives cannot be met, the System Retirement Policy should be amended and re-issued.

> **Hint**
>
> Whether you consult with the Data Store Owner and Business Domain Expert on each change to a System Retirement Policy, or 'bulk up' the changes for one big session is a matter of judgement influenced by local factors. I like to feel that at this stage I am sufficiently familiar with the Legacy Data Stores and Data Store Owner preferences to be able to judge if a change is significant or not and therefore prefer to bulk up changes into sets of changes. But if in doubt, always remember Golden Rule 1 and ask.

The System Retirement Policy will now contain all the requirements that have to be met for the Legacy Data Store in question to be removed or archived. It will contain, in enterprise-intelligible language, a description of the technical solution proposal that fulfils these requirements. It will explain what data will be migrated, what will not be migrated and what will happen to data that is not migrated. It will contain Data Transitional Rules as necessary to deal with the actions the Business Domain Expert must take over the migration period. It will describe the user's view of Transient Data Stores.

Sign-off

There is often a temptation to put before the Data Store Owner a big fat document of all the program specifications, technical specifications and System Retirement Policies and ask them to sign off the equivalent of the New York telephone directory. Usually they are given a couple of days to do this. I do not believe that this is fair or useful. Having technical specifications reviewed by non-technical staff does not increase their accuracy, nor does it ultimately protect the project if there are any flaws but it can lead to the mutual recriminations that this process is striving to avoid. I therefore recommend the review and sign-off in table 12.1.

Anecdote

It is all very well for me to say go for a limited sign off, but we have all worked in politically charged environments where there is a perceived need for everyone to sign off everything. I was consulting to a large financial institution where the sign-off list for some documents ran to two pages. The net result was that very few documents ever came out of a draft state. I spent hours in fruitless meetings where impatient technicians tried to explain arcane technical complexities to bored executives. But if you have done your team building right in Stage 1 and Stage 2 then you will get through this perhaps a little easier than where the atmosphere is soured by mutual ignorance and mistrust.

TABLE 12.1 *Reviewing and sign-off allocation*

Document	Reviewers	Sign-off
Data migration timetable	Data Store Owners Business Domain Experts Technical Data Experts Programme Experts Programme management	Data Store Owners Programme management
Data Migration Technical Specification	Technical Data Experts Programme Experts Developers	Technical Data Experts Programme Experts Lead developer
Transient Data Store specifications	Technical Data Experts Programme Experts	Technical Data Experts Programme Experts

TABLE 12.1 *Continued*

Document	Reviewers	Sign-off
	Developers	Lead Developer
	Business Domain Experts[1]	Data Store Owners[1]
	Data Store Owners[1]	
Amendments to Legacy Data Store specifications	Data Store Owners	Data Store Owners
	Technical Data Experts	Technical Data Experts
	Programme Experts	Programme Experts
	Developers	Lead developer
	Business Domain Experts	
Fallback specification	Data Store Owners	Data Store Owners
	Business Domain Experts	Programme management
	Technical Data Experts	
	Programme Experts	
	Programme management	
System Retirement Policies	Data Store Owners	Data Store Owners
	Business Domain Experts	Programme management
	Technical Data Experts	
	Programme Experts	
	other Data Stakeholders as appropriate[2]	

1 Only where the Transient Data Store is to be used by people outside of the programme and only from an ergonomic perspective.
2 eg Audit and Regulatory Experts, Data Customers, Corporate Data Architects – but only where they have a valid, compelling interest.

Recursion

Physical design and build is always a very recursive process. Testing throws up problems with the timetable, changes to programs create changes in System Retirement Policies and Data Transitional Rules. Allow time in your planning for going back and reworking deliverables at least once.

STEP 3.2: DATA MIGRATION TESTING

Once again I am going to say at this point that I am not going to try to teach you about the different stages of testing. Not least because testing strategies and quality assurance in general have filled more pages in more volumes than I can do justice to here. I am anticipating that the probable reader of this book will be as familiar with testing as I am.

So if we are all so good at testing why is it that so many projects have problems with the final, migrated, result? Usually after it is in production?

Hopefully I will have answered some of questions above. Typically we get it wrong because:

- we make assumptions about the data sources;
- we make assumptions about data quality;
- we make assumptions about what is meant by data quality;
- we underestimate the knowledge in the enterprise;
- we assume leadership in an area where we lack knowledge.

In short, we ignore the four Golden Rules! If you have followed the activities outlined above you will have avoided these traps.

- You will have chosen the most appropriate data sources in the light of the Data Stakeholders' knowledge.
- You will know in detail what the enterprise means by 'data quality'.
- You will have metrics that tell you what your remaining data quality issues are.
- The knowledge in the enterprise will be bound into the Data Quality Rules and System Retirement Policies you have created.
- The enterprise will have been leading the data migration project from start to finish.

We are now entering the final lap. Get this testing right and, short of acts of God, everything will go right in your migration.

Using System Retirement Policies in testing

Not surprisingly, the System Retirement Policies are, after the extract, transform and load definitions, the most important single set of documents that you have to steer your test strategy.

From the System Retirement Policies you will know what it is that your Data Stakeholders consider important and how to measure it.

Make sure you plan to test for it.

From the Data Quality Rules exercises you will also know how far the enterprise was prepared to go in correcting the data. Do not expect it to be any better after you have manipulated it.

> **Hint**
>
> During the build phase new people (usually coders of one type or another but also professional testers) come into the data migration project. They will not have been through the whole process and may not be familiar with your enterprise-centric approach. They are often tempted to reassert the old technology-led paradigm. But beware – this is not the moment to attempt to polish the data any more than has been agreed. The

> **risks usually outweigh the benefits. Educate your new staff. If, of course, they see a real showstopper that the rest of you have missed, then you have to react by initiating a new Data Quality Rule process, but resist tinkering!**

Look for a Reality Check

You will have checked that the relational integrity rules have been observed. You will have checked the data by type and by length and by value range. You will have done all that the validation software is capable of. But how can the Data Store Owners and Business Domain Experts be certain that the data in the new system matches the reality on the ground? The answer, of course, is that you will have already asked them!

When I say 'asked them' I mean asked them the question 'How will you be certain, before we switch the new system on (and the old system off), that the data in it matches the reality as you experience it?' Get them to tackle this first-order question, not to answer a series of second-order questions that you devise (like 'Is this the number of stores in our company?' or 'Does this sample of customers have the right name and address?'). In other words, what are their acceptance criteria? And these conversations should have occurred and been recorded and signed off at the inception of the project when the System Retirement Policies were first created. Back then, when the demise of their core production systems was but a distant possibility, you got them to commit to the general scope of reassurance they would need.

So all of this should be covered in the System Retirement Policies but it is worthwhile reviewing it with the Data Store Owners and Business Domain Experts. This is not an invitation to rework Data Quality Rule and System Retirement Policy assumptions that were agreed in Stage 1 and Stage 2, however. Any change to this initial scope needs to go through the most exacting change control mechanism you can devise because it is likely to seriously damage programme outcomes. This is about the mechanics of getting data quality information in front of Data Stakeholders, in such a way that they can prove that its accuracy has not been inadvertently degraded in the migration process beyond that which was agreed in the Data Quality Rules. What reports do they need? Do they need some form of Transient Data Store? How can this be fitted in within the time scales of the wider programme?

As a project professional you should guide the discussion in terms of what types of testing are tenable and appropriate in your environment. A final set of Data Quality Rules exercises will be performed to test the accuracy of the migration.

> **Hint**
>
> At this point it is tempting to give in to the pressure of your peers and rename this final set of Data Quality Rules 'user acceptance testing' or whatever it is called in your project methodology. I try to resist this, at least external to the programme. Your key Data Stakeholders will have been through at least two iterations of Data Quality Rules activities. This is not the time to change the nomenclature on them.

STEP 3.3: BUILDING THE MIGRATION SOFTWARE

Yet again this is not the book to lecture you on how to build suitable software, how to control changes to it, how to unit and system test it. You will have plenty of experience of this. I only have a couple of observations to make in connection with data migration projects.

Overengineering the solution

Most software engineers, bless them, want to build quality software. It is in their blood. For a data migration exercise, good enough is quite good enough. It is much better that software be delivered earlier, tested according to the test strategy, and working, than late but polished to a level of technical sophistication that would dazzle a visiting professor from MIT. I am not suggesting that you encourage your coders to cut corners, but gnarly software that makes maximum use of available utilities is much better than super-sophisticated hand-crafted code. Don't forget that this software is a one-use product. It will be thrown away once the project is over.

Data Stakeholder involvement

Where the solution involves the creation of Transient Data Stores, a joint application development approach pays dividends. The solution should be driven by the specification but its ergonomics can be greatly enhanced by involving the Business Domain Expert.

STEP 3.4: EXECUTE THE MIGRATION

Step 3.4.0: step initiation

This is the moment the whole project, maybe the whole programme, has been building up to. It is so important that it merits its own step initiation phase.

You should have:

- a full set of System Retirement Policies, signed off as being complete;
- Data Transitional Rules signed off and briefed out;
- a data migration timetable;
- a set of load programs or scripts tested and ready;
- Data Stakeholders primed and ready to answer any queries;
- Legacy Data Stores and Transient Data Stores with data of sufficient quality to migrate;
- the non-functional aspects agreed, installed and ready for action.

Check them off. Make especially sure that the wider enterprise understands, and is ready to enact, the Data Transitional Rules. Create entries in the risk register for any items that have not been completed and get the Data Store Owners to sign off the mitigation steps in the System Retirement Policies.

Step 3.4.1: go live

If you have followed this book to the letter, the above will naturally be in place. All that remains to do then is to give it your final sign-off and stand back and let it happen! Easy, eh?

> **Hint**
>
> There is always so much focus on this last couple of weeks that you rarely have any problems attracting the attention of management to any issues you might encounter. The chief worry I find is that all the highly motivated, highly skilled labour that has been working on the project so far is suddenly freed up and can offer you 'assistance'. Once again you have the problem of resisting reversion to a technologist-led solution. The answer to this is to have written a strong, well-endorsed data migration strategy to start off with, then to have stuck to it. Also, if you have built strong links with the Programme Experts this will help fend off unwelcome attentions. But be prepared for it to happen. Data migration may be uninteresting to 90% of the programme for 90% of the timeline, but come that last 10% you become quite fascinating!

OK then, maybe not quite so easy, but you are prepared. You have a plan and you have briefed out that plan. Your virtual team of technical and non-technical resources are ready and you have a named resource to call on, whatever the type of query.

Once more I cannot in this book cover the shape of your particular migration. Will it take a week, or a month or just a few hours to complete?

Will you be running in parallel for an interim period or will it be a once-and-for-all changeover? Does it involve many complex steps to repoint interfaces etc or is it pretty much a straight swap, one system for another?

> **Hint**
>
> This is probably teaching grandma how to suck eggs but at the risk of being patronizing, always in your migration planning have a Fallback position that you can restore to if catastrophe overtakes you. In the context of data migration planning make sure the Fallback is sanctioned by the Data Store Owners in advance, that you and they know the criterion that triggers the Fallback, and make sure Data Transitional Rules have been agreed (if not necessarily briefed out). If you are called on to abort a migration and you have decided against pre-briefing the emergency Data Transitional Rules, make sure there is a mechanism ready to brief these rules out quickly.

Whatever the shape of your migration, it is always an exciting time. If you have followed the precepts in this book it will be exciting not stressful. I would advise you to enjoy it. Look forward to seeing the culmination of all that hard work going through its paces like a thoroughbred racehorse. And share that excitement with your key Data Stakeholders. Phone them up, congratulate them on their effort, celebrate the success with them. It may not be you, but it sure as hell benefits the next project technician down the pike that has to deal with them!

STEP 3.5: POST-IMPLEMENTATION REVIEW

We all pay lip service to this. It is a statement in most project plans that we will conduct a post-project review. How often they really happen is more of a moot point.

But in a data migration exercise they have an additional role to the 'lessons learnt' and 'would have been better if' statements. There are some activities that *must* happen after a data migration and some that are just darn useful.

Step 3.5.1: mopping up

We would like it if all the planned data that was expected to be loaded was loaded but it rarely happens that way.

Some data will have been knowingly left out because of pressure of time or other reasons it could not be corrected in time. The Data Quality Rules will have prepared for this but something may still have to be done with it.

Some data will not have loaded for unforeseen reasons at system load time. Fortunately for the project, because you have been working with the Data Store Owners and Business Domain Experts for months or years beforehand, they are trained up to making rapid decisions about data quality standards – what they can live with, what is serious but not fatal and what is a showstopper. You will have jointly created Data Quality Rules on the fly, made a record of them, maybe issued Data Transitional Rules to cope with the problem whilst it is fixed post-implementation. Now is the time in the post-implementation lull to review these items and amplify the Data Quality Rules to deal with them. It may be that the new data quality threshold is deemed acceptable; it may be that an exercise of data cleansing is authorized. Either way, this is now the time to hand this over to the post-implementation team to control.

> **Hint**
>
> All projects must come to an end and this one is no exception. I always try to get agreement at the start of a project to an agreed length of post-implementation time for mopping up, but this time must be fixed. Anything that will span beyond this period must become part of a separate project.

Step 3.5.2: implementing System Retirement Policies

Not all systems can be switched off in line with the implementation of the new system because of overhanging transactions etc. The System Retirement Policies will indicate when each Legacy Data Store should be decommissioned. Make sure that these activities take place. We do not want to leave phantom systems around undermining the credibility of the new system. This is a point on which you have to be ruthless.

Step 3.5.3: ongoing data quality enhancement

You will have built up, over the course of Stages 1 and 2 the skills in the business to engage in structured data quality enhancement. This is something the business can carry out under their own steam. Of course they will not have the support of a sophisticated technical operative like yourself but they can address some of the data issues that you maybe lacked time for, by departmentally commissioned Data Quality Rules initiatives. Always leave it as a suggestion with the Data Store Owners.

STAGE 3 PROJECT CONTROLS

Standard 'design – build – test' rules can be employed to plan the effort required. The specification will be available either in a single document or as part of the System Retirement Policies, Data Quality Rules and mapping documents.

There may be ongoing Data Quality Rules work taking place and this can run right up to new system go live. Data Transitional Rules may be in place or will have been specified in the System Retirement Policies. A consolidated design is required and this may involve updating System Retirement Policies if clashes or technical problems intervene. Once the design is finalized this should be reflected in the System Retirement Policies and their sign-off is the green light from the business that systems can be migrated and Legacy Data Stores decommissioned. On the new system side the load specification should be signed-off at least by the new system Data Store Owner, but more usually by the programme technical experts, programme manager, programme sponsor... well you should know the signatories in your organization.

You are then free to go ahead with the data migration build and test. Any data problems, and if we have done our jobs properly there should not be any, need to be documented. You will need to create a new Data Quality Rules document for them at post-implementation review time. They may also impact on the System Retirement Policies, which may need updating. This involves going back to the business for consultation. However, by now your virtual team will be ready and willing to supply answers, which is useful because problems at this stage need prompt fixes, not long-winded discussion

How far the data migration team is involved in go live planning itself varies from project to project. Our run times and system requirements certainly inform the process, but there are other commercial, logistic and human resource issues that generally go beyond the scope of data migration. However, the System Retirement Policies should tell us what is acceptable and what is not. Our relationships with our key Data Stakeholders mean that we are better able to inform the planning process and conclude a dialogue acceptable to all Data Stakeholders.

Chapter review

In this chapter we have covered the build, test and run activities that constitute the completion of a data migration project. We have seen how System Retirement Policies, Data Quality Rules and extract, transform and load definitions combine with our relationship with the Data Stakeholders to create a seamless flow into go live .

We have also seen what processes are required post implementation, including the enactment of the System Retirement Policies.

Part Three
Rescuing Data Migration Projects

13 Data Migration Projects That Have Gone Wrong: A Survival Guide

This chapter gives you a step-by-step guide to straightening out flawed data migration projects.

This chapter makes use of concepts introduced earlier in the book and you are advised to re-read those sections as appropriate.

INTRODUCTION

First of all you have my sympathy. But be of good hope. This is not an isolated incident. At least half my career has been spent parachuting into data migration projects that have gone wrong and trying to get them up and running again.

There are three phases of activity that need to be worked through:

- **Stabilization:** Stopping the situation getting worse, getting on top of the firefighting and creating an environment where a more considered approach can be adopted.

- **Planned activity:** Working in a more controlled way through a series of releases or iterations that will deliver measurable and perceivable improvements to the situation.

- **Post-implementation mop-up:** Taking care of those things that, in a well-delivered migration, would have been completed as a matter of course but that in the present circumstances are probably best put on the back burner.

Anecdote

Typical of my experience was the well-known high street name that was two years into a six-month migration project. The management were making a last ditch effort to get something delivered. At the same time the lawyers were being consulted with a view to suing the principal supplier. It all looked very messy and about to get even messier in public.

> Fortunately, common sense prevailed and a staged migration was achieved, but only after a significant amount of pain.

STABILIZATION

Your first task is to stabilize the situation. There is often the temptation to just carry on doing more of whatever you were doing before. Resist it! Follow the points below to get out of the mire and back onto the sunny uplands of a well-managed migration project:

1. Read this book. Come on now, I know that in panic, or desperate hope, you have picked this book up and gone straight to this chapter. I know I would. Well, you need to understand the Golden Rules and the key concepts covered in the first couple of chapters. OK, maybe the rest of the book you can skim over, but when I start talking about Data Stakeholders and Data Quality Rules it will help if you understand where I am coming from.

2. Buy some time to replan. The urge to 'do something' is as understandable as it is misplaced. The project will almost certainly have compromised Golden Rules 1 and 2. You need a plan that will get the enterprise back in charge and the technologists back in their supporting role. You need to communicate that plan out to all the interested parties.

    A useful way of getting this time is to enact the following two steps immediately. They are necessary and will almost certainly have been overlooked. But use all the political clout you can muster to reappraise where you are and how you get to where you need to be.

> ### Hint
>
> A direct approach is unlikely to be successful at this point. If the enterprise has ceded responsibility for the success of the migration to the technologists they are unlikely to rush to re-embrace that responsibility when it is all going wrong. A little more subtlety is required that will draw the enterprise into the ownership roles. The best you may achieve will be that they are willing to lead, but not to accept formal responsibility. See below for some ideas on how to achieve this.

3. Get the list of Legacy Data Stores under formal change control. I have never arrived on a data migration that is under threat of failure where all the potential Legacy Data Stores are documented and

under control. Often the programme has succumbed to the group-think that the major Legacy Data Store being replaced is the only source of data. As the section on Legacy Data Stores shows, this is almost never the case. Do not allow the fact that one major Legacy Data Store is under formal change control blind you to the requirement to catalogue all the minor ones. It is at this point of crisis that you may have the best chance of convincing the power brokers in the enterprise that the project has to be allowed to look further afield for valid data items. You will almost certainly not have time to complete a formal analysis of Key Business Data Areas or Legacy Data Store to the degree of rigour one would like, but each potential Legacy Data Store needs to be identified, assessed and placed under change control.

> **Hint**
>
> **You will at this stage be confronted with a bunch of irritating Business Domain Experts and Data Store Owners all saying 'I told you so'. This is to be welcomed. Do not be defensive. Used with intelligence and sensitivity this can be a lever to reinstate the business as the controllers and owners of the migration process. Golden Rules 1 and 2 will almost certainly have been violated – or else why are you in this mess? Put your hands up and say 'mea culpa' (or 'Yeh, you're right, we are responsible' if your Latin isn't up to it), then add 'But now *we* are in this mess how do *we* get out of it?'. Get the enterprise to share responsibility for the solution if not for the problem.**

4. Get the list of outstanding issues under formal change control and start creating Data Quality Rules documents for them. All well-run projects will be maintaining an issues register but often it will only be for the most significant issues that need to be considered at programme board level. So you may or may not find the individual data migration issues logged. Either way, it is time to get the programme to rethink along Data Quality Rules lines. Because each data issue needs a Data Quality Rule and each Data Quality Rule needs a Data Store Owner and a Business Domain Expert, it starts to get you out amongst the enterprise seeking solutions.

5. Create your own key Data Stakeholder list. There is no getting away from it. If you are going to rescue the project you need the help of the people who know both the data and the correct order of prioritization. Unfortunately this list may be something that is best kept within the confines of the project. You will be wasting your time

trying to get formal sign-up to all the responsibilities of Data Store Ownership with a visible disaster awaiting the recipient. I know I would not willingly take on that responsibility. Would you? And remember the analogy of the train ride and the quest. You are at risk of changing metaphors on your key Data Stakeholders. So although you must know who the key Data Stakeholders are, use a little subtlety in getting them to own the solution.

6. Stop fixing and start consulting. Rein in the reaction to fix every problem as soon as it appears. You will not have time for the formal gap analysis proposed in Stage 2 of the strategy illustration. You will have suffered considerable agony as your project trips up over the bigger data gaps that you did not find out about in time. Learn from the pain. Explain that the process will be iterative. Accept that you are in the unenviable position of not knowing where all the data gaps lie. Expect to find more as you go along and plan for it.

PLANNED ACTIVITY

Once you have completed steps 1 to 6 above and have a better feel for the shape of the problem you will be in a position to put together a plan that will involve the correct Data Stakeholders in Data Quality Rules and prioritization exercises. The plan will inevitably be iterative and release based. So:

7. From the created fault log, start prioritizing the faults and create realistic estimates of how long they will take to correct.

8. Institute a tight release and configuration management strategy. In the hurly-burly of a struggling implementation there is always the temptation to bypass normal controls and fix things on the fly. Once you become aware of previously fixed bugs reappearing you will know that your configuration management policies are compromised (that is if you have any, of course). Step in before this happens – it hugely discredits any deployment exercise. The published releases will tell the business what is being fixed and which releases they will be in. The components of each release must be under the control of the key Data Stakeholders, both within the programme and within the enterprise. Set up a suitable forum where these decisions can be made.

> **Hint**
>
> In these circumstances I usually institute a weekly release strategy with a weekly meeting of key Data Stakeholders to agree the release policy. Once the major

issues are resolved this can become fortnightly, monthly etc. Extreme formality is required. The releases should be documented in terms of the Data Quality Rules they implement, the date they will be implemented and given a formal release number. Keep the meetings focussed and short! Less than one hour is best. They are not designed to fix the problems but to prioritize the solutions.

I also institute the use of proper configuration management tools if these are not being used. But the tools only work where there is discipline in place.

9. Be aware of Golden Rule 3. You are now very much at risk of loading that which is expedient as opposed to that which is necessary. It may be that for political or practical reasons less than optimum data needs to be released but more than ever you need compromises led by the enterprise and accepted by the enterprise. If less than optimum data is released, do you have a plan for correcting it in a later iteration? Has the reason been sufficiently well communicated to the other Data Stakeholders?

The situation should now be under control. I am not saying that you will be popular with the programme sponsors or the enterprise or even that you will hit your deadlines, but you will have a rolling release plan that will inform the enterprise of when a stable deliverable of acceptable quality will be reached. You will be managing via Data Quality Rules. These are designed to be built up into plans. You will be identifying your key Data Stakeholders and bringing them into the project to lead prioritization decisions.

POST-IMPLEMENTATION MOP-UP

With:

- Data Quality Rules covering the known data gaps;
- key Data Stakeholders recognized and given due control over the data migration process;
- Legacy Data Stores catalogued to cover some of the data gaps; and
- an iterative release management strategy in place

it is time to look at the other items that you will not have had time for.

System Retirement Policies

You will not have prepared System Retirement Policies. It is unlikely, given the time pressures you are under, that you will have time to create them either. It is far easier to open discussions about system retirement at the start of a project when the prospect of it happening is some time hence than when the Data Store Owners are faced with the imminent demise of their Legacy Data Stores. Compound this natural instinct to conservatism in the face of change with the calamitous situation facing the data migration project and we shouldn't be surprised that any sensible person will want to hang on to existing certainties with long clingy arms! But Legacy Data Stores do have to be closed down. I usually content myself with raising this on the programme issue log and making sure that it gets taken up as part of the post-implementation review. It really comes down to least worst case activity. Initiated early enough, System Retirement Policies tie in Data Store Owners to the migration process. Initiated at this stage they distract, antagonize and scare, so you should probably not attempt to do them.

Key Business Data Areas

If you are parachuted into the middle of a failing data migration project, there is rarely time to re-decompose the problem into sensible Key Business Data Areas. The force of necessity will have created obvious decompositions of activity, usually centred on physical data stores. You will have to decide if what you gain by repartitioning activities around a more data-centric division, in terms of clarity of analysis, will compensate for the time and disturbance it takes. In my experience, unless management can be persuaded to accept a substantial postponement, you are better off settling for what you find. You will, however, be aware that because you have inadequate analysis to work from, you are running the risk of discovering more external consistency problems (ie problems of consistency across multiple Legacy Data Stores). Raise a formal risk on the programme's risk register and as mitigation point to the additional iterations in the new migration plan.

Reality Check

In most cases there is no time at all to perform Reality Checks for the data you are trying to load. Use the new Legacy Data Stores and Business Domain Experts unearthed in the stabilization phase to look for existing data stores or enterprise knowledge that might corroborate the fact that the items being loaded correspond to real things out there in the business. Be especially alert to what the Business Domain Experts are saying. Again, log this as a risk, the mitigation being the closeness you have to the Business Domain Experts. If matching the data to existing business reality becomes an issue there may be nothing that you can do about it at this late stage. Just bear in mind Golden Rule 3 and get the appropriate Data Stakeholder to assess the need for remedial action post implementation. One of the benefits of introducing the enterprise to the use of Data Quality Rules, albeit at a late stage, is that you are introducing them to a corrective mechanism that can be used post implementation. It is a question of getting the Data Quality Rule process embedded in the culture and successfully transferring ownership of ongoing data quality from the programme to the enterprise.

CONCLUSION

Like a large ocean liner, when a programme is heading in the wrong direction it takes considerable effort to turn it around. In the case of data migration projects that are going wrong there will be a huge weight of misplaced expectations and misunderstandings to overcome. It is more important than ever that the four Golden Rules are obeyed, but preaching them enterprise-wide may be counterproductive.

The enterprise, generally excluded in failing migrations, needs to be brought back to the centre of the solution, quality improvements must be measurable and data quality compromises made that are acceptable both to the enterprise and to the programme – all in the context of a tense and conflict-ridden atmosphere where recriminations are never far away.

I wish you the best of luck.

> ### Chapter review
>
> *In this chapter I have covered:*
> - *nine steps that will get your project back on track;*
> - *a list of those desirables that you will probably have to jettison at least in the short term;*
> - *hints as to how you can recover some of those things that you should have to hand but probably don't.*

Index

BCS products and services

Other products and services from the British Computer Society that might be of interest to you include:

Publishing

BCS publications, including books, magazine and peer-reviewed journals provide readers with informed content on business, management, legal and emerging technological issues, supporting the professional, academic and practical needs of the IT community. Subjects covered include business process management, IT law for managers and transition management. www.bcs.org/publications

BCS professional products and services

The BCS promotes the use of the SFIA*plus* IT skills framework, which forms the basis of a range of professional development products and services for both individual practitioners and employers. This includes BCS Skills*Manager* and BCS Career*Developer*. www.bcs.org/products

Qualifications

Information Systems Examination Board (ISEB) qualifications are the industry standard both in the UK and abroad. With over 100,000 practitioners now qualified, it is proof of the popularity of the qualifications. These qualifications ensure that IT professionals develop the skills, knowledge and confidence to perform to their full potential. There is a huge range on offer, covering all major areas of IT. In essence, ISEB qualifications are for forward-looking individuals and companies who want to stay ahead and who are serious about driving business forward. www.iseb.org.uk

BCS professional examinations are examined to the academic level of a UK honours degree and are the essential qualifications for a career in computing and IT. Whether you seek greater job recognition, promotion or a new career direction, you will find that BCS professional examinations are internationally recognized, flexible and suited to the needs of the IT industry. www.bcs.org/exams

The European Certification of IT Professionals (EUCIP) is aimed at IT professionals and practitioners wishing to gain professional certification and competency development. www.bcs.org/eucip

European Computer Driving Licence (ECDL) is the internationally recognized computer skills qualification that enables people to demonstrate their competence in computer skills. ECDL is managed in the UK by the BCS. ECDL Advanced has been introduced to take computer skills certification to the next level and teaches extensive knowledge of particular computing tools. www.ecdl.co.uk

Networking and events

BCS's specialist groups and branches provide excellent professional networking opportunities by keeping members abreast of latest developments, discussing topical issues and making useful contacts. www.bcs.org/bcs/groups

The society's programme of social events, lectures, awards schemes and competitions provides more opportunities to network. www.bcs.org/events

Further information

This information was correct at the time of publication but could change in the future. For the latest information, please contact:

The British Computer Society
First Floor, Block D
North Star House
North Star Avenue
Swindon SN2 1FA
UK

Telephone: 0845 300 4417 (UK only) or +44 1793 417424 (overseas)
Email: customerservice@hq.bcs.org.uk
Web: www.bcs.org

Learning Resources
Centre